Information Systems Engineering Library

# Estimating on an SSADM Project

LONDON: HMSO

**Acknowledgements**

The assistance of Nick Hardie, Jeet Khaira and Paul Turner, under contract to CCTA from BIS Information Systems Ltd is gratefully acknowledged.

The assistance of Model Systems Ltd and the Union Bank of Switzerland is also gratefully acknowledged.

© **Crown copyright 1994**   Applications for reproduction should be made to HMSO

ISBN: 0 11 330631 8

**For further information regarding CCTA products please contact:**

CCTA Library
Rosebery Court
St Andrews Business Park
Norwich
NR7 0HS
01 603 704704

# Foreword

**The Information Systems Engineering Library** provides guidance on managing and carrying out Information Systems Engineering activities. In the IS life cycle, Information Systems Engineering takes place once the IS strategy has been defined. It is concerned with the development and ongoing improvement of information systems up to the operational stage, and their maintenance whilst in operational use.

The Information Systems Engineering Library complements other CCTA products, in particular the project management method, PRINCE, and the systems analysis and design method, SSADM.

Volumes in the Information Systems Engineering Library are of interest to varying levels of staff from IS directors to IS providers, helping them to improve the quality and productivity of their IS development work. Some volumes in this library should also be of interest to business managers, IS users and those involved in market testing, whose business operations depend on having effective IS support by means of Information Systems Engineering activities.

The Information Systems Engineering Library also complements other related CCTA publications particularly the Programme and Project Management Library, the Information Management Library for data management issues, the IT Infrastructure Library for operational issues and the IS Planning Subject Guides for strategic issues.

CCTA welcomes customer views on Information Systems Engineering Library publications. Please send your comments to:

Information Systems Engineering Group
Rosebery Court
St Andrews Business Park
NORWICH
NR7 0HS

Estimating on an SSADM Project

# Contents

| Chapter | | page |
|---|---|---|
| 1 | **Introduction** | 7 |
| | 1.1 Purpose | |
| | 1.2 Who should read this volume | |
| | 1.3 Structure of this volume | |
| 2 | **Overview of estimating** | 11 |
| | 2.1 Context of estimating | |
| | 2.2 Definition of estimating | |
| | 2.3 Why estimate? | |
| | 2.4 Problems with estimating | |
| | 2.5 Levels of confidence in estimating | |
| | 2.6 Who should estimate? | |
| 3 | **Estimating methods** | 17 |
| | 3.1 Project Model and System Model | |
| | 3.2 Stages | |
| | 3.3 Tactics | |
| | 3.4 Techniques | |
| | 3.5 Best practice | |
| 4 | **Issues affecting estimates and estimators** | 33 |
| | 4.1 Factors to be considered in estimating | |
| | 4.2 System and project characteristics | |
| | 4.3 Projects database | |
| | 4.4 Causes of bad estimates | |
| | 4.5 Need for honesty and integrity | |
| 5 | **Estimating procedures (general)** | 39 |
| | 5.1 Basic procedure | |
| | 5.2 Documentation and change control | |
| | 5.3 Project, module and stage estimating | |
| | 5.4 Software support | |
| 6 | **Developing estimates for SSADM projects** | 51 |
| | 6.1 Introduction to suggested procedure | |
| | 6.2 Project activities and considerations | |
| | 6.3 Principles and procedures | |
| | 6.4 When to estimate in SSADM Version 4 | |

| | | |
|---|---|---|
| 7 | **Estimating SSADM Version 4 projects using a spreadsheet**<br>7.1 Introduction<br>7.2 Using the spreadsheet<br>7.3 Input from the Project Initiation Document<br>7.4 Initial parameters<br>7.5 Project complexity<br>7.6 Project adjustment factor<br>7.7 Spreadsheet | 57 |
| 8 | **Estimating SSADM Version 4 projects using the Mk II Function Point Analysis spreadsheet**<br>8.1 Introduction<br>8.2 Overview of the Mk II Function Point estimating method<br>8.3 Assembling the inputs for the FPA spreadsheet<br>8.4 Step by step guide to the FPA spreadsheet | 69 |
| Annex A | **Estimating points and scope** | 83 |
| Annex B | **Estimating points** | 85 |
| Annex C | **Estimating spreadsheet** | 87 |
| Annex D | **Mk II Function Point Analysis spreadsheet** | 93 |
| | **Bibliography** | 99 |
| | **Glossary** | 101 |

Chapter 1
Introduction

# 1 Introduction

**1.1 Purpose**

Effective project management requires the ability to estimate the amount of work, the resources and the timescale needed to meet project objectives. The purpose of this volume is to give advice on estimating IS development projects using SSADM Version 4, and to state where estimating can be used in SSADM. The volume also gives an introduction to the terms used in the estimating process but is not intended as a training aid either for SSADM or for estimating. It is intended to complement and, where necessary, to supplement an organization's existing estimating practice. It covers the general principles and methods of estimating as well as SSADM specifics.

**1.2 Who should read this volume**

The volume is aimed at a variety of interest groups:

- **IT Managers** are provided with a set of principles and recommended practice to help in formulating, with their Project Managers and SSADM practitioners, the detailed methods for estimating that will be used on projects under their control

- **SSADM Practitioners** are furnished with a general orientation to project estimating principles and practice, and specific guidelines to help them in formulating project estimates

- **Project Managers** will find a recommendation of best practice for SSADM projects that can be used as it stands, or adapted for local needs, to ensure commonality of approach across projects. A survey of estimating methods is also provided

- **IT Estimating and Metrics Teams** have a framework to support the establishment and maintenance of standard estimating practice, thus enabling meaningful metrics to be collected to enhance the accuracy of future project estimates

- **User Management** will find it helpful in explaining the basis upon which IT Directorates and other IS providers submit costings and schedules for proposed projects at the Feasibility Study Stage, and for current projects in subsequent stages.

### 1.3 Structure of this volume

The volume is structured as follows:

- Chapter 2 provides an overview of what estimating is, its rationale and key principles; essentially it explains *why* estimating should be carried out.

- Chapter 3 is an introduction to the methods employed in estimating – the broad approaches, particular techniques and general best practice; it aims to explain *how* estimating is carried out.

- Chapter 4 addresses the issues to be considered by estimators, their managers and clients – factors to be allowed for, pitfalls that may be encountered; essentially, *what* estimating must take into account.

- Chapter 5 sets down recommended estimating practice, and a generic step by step procedure for formulating estimates; it also provides some considerations for automated support for estimating.

- Chapter 6 builds on the preceding three chapters to provide guidelines and procedures for estimating specifically for SSADM Version 4 projects, including where in the development life cycle to estimate and the factors relevant to estimating at those various points.

- Chapter 7 describes how to use the SSADM Version 4 estimating method and supporting spreadsheet in Annex C.

- Chapter 8 describes how to use the spreadsheet in Annex D to support the use of Mk II Function Point Analysis when estimating an SSADM Version 4 project.

- Annexes A & B describe Estimating Points.

Chapter 1
Introduction

There is also a Glossary of estimating terms used throughout the volume.

**1.4 Assumed knowledge** This volume is written with the assumption that readers are familiar with SSADM. Those not familiar with SSADM terminology may have to consult with SSADM experts or refer to the SSADM manuals.

## Estimating on an SSADM Project

# 2 Overview of estimating

This chapter gives an overview of what the volume is setting out to cover: the essential issues in project management that are addressed by the implementation and practice of effective estimating.

## 2.1 Context of estimating

Effective project management is an objective of any organization. Any project should be planned, and planning includes estimating. But more broadly, estimating is one element of the whole iterative process of project planning and control which includes:

- information gathering
- estimation of effort, skills, resources and timescales
- planning and scheduling
- monitoring and control
- reporting.

All these aspects have to be addressed in a successful implementation of project management.

Estimates are the initial input into planning and scheduling. For an IS development project the aim of estimating, planning and scheduling is to determine, based on limited information which progressively increases during the project:

- the cost of a system
- when it can be delivered
- the likelihood of achieving the said cost and delivery date.

SSADM's modular structure and product oriented approach provide a good foundation for estimating.

## 2.2 Definition of estimating

Estimating can be defined as follows:

*The process of determining the amount of work, resource and timescale required to achieve the development of a product or system to an agreed level of quality and functionality, and of assessing the degree of risk and uncertainty associated with the amount determined.*

Project costs can be derived from such estimates, with allowance made for costs such as hardware costs, fixed costs and overheads, depending upon the nature of the project.

Estimation is initially of effort required. Effort estimates are translated to timescale estimates as part of project planning through the application of appropriate resource to the estimates of the effort required. But estimators may also attach timescale as well as effort estimates to particular tasks. These timescale estimates will often be based on similar projects using a similar development approach.

## 2.3 Why estimate?

Management and technical staff should have a clear idea of why it is necessary to produce estimates and for what purpose they will be used. Estimates are produced to:

- decide practical completion dates for projects

- enable the calculation of stage and project cost so as to assess the viability of the project, both at the Feasibility Study Stage and on an on-going basis, particularly at the end of project stages or SSADM modules

- enable identification of impossible targets

- enable appropriate planning of personnel and other resources to be carried out

- enable agreement on budgets

- allow management to make reasoned decisions

- gain management commitment

# Chapter 2
## Overview of estimating

- assist personnel motivation by setting targets

- track actuals against estimates for management purposes and for calculation of future estimates.

### 2.4 Problems with estimating

Organizations traditionally have problems with estimating because of:

- unrealistic expectations as to the accuracy of estimates

- the lack of experienced estimators and appropriate methods and tools

- wide variation of estimating methods

- poor records of previous IS developments and estimates for them

- a failure to take account of changes in development environments and approaches

- a lack of separation of estimating from scheduling

- the absence of a consistent defined estimating approach for the organization

- lack of training in estimating

- refusal by management to accept inconvenient estimates.

This volume aims to support organizations in addressing these problems with particular emphasis on estimating in an SSADM environment.

### 2.5 Levels of confidence in estimating

Estimating is not easy and since most systems development projects involve elements of technical or commercial risk and uncertainty about details of the project, cost and time overruns can occur even on the most strictly managed project. A practical approach to estimating that gives as accurate an estimate as possible is therefore required. It must take account of the uncertainty and risk factors affecting the project:

- uncertainty results from inadequate detailed information about a project and the system it aims to produce. Uncertainty should decrease as the project progresses

- risk results from factors such as system complexity and organizational experience of the application under development. Risk may be incurred quite separately from uncertainty; that is to say, project and system requirements may be well understood, but risks may still attach to their realization.

The presence of either or both uncertainty and risk makes it essential to put ranges or percentage confidence levels on estimates.

Some of the reasons for uncertainty and risk in the estimating process are discussed in Chapter 4.

Initial estimates are required for project level plans to enable management to sanction work to go ahead. These first, 'provisional' estimates (produced by a Feasibility Study, or at the start of a project) are prone to a wide margin of error, due to uncertainty about project and system details; projects have all too often exceeded their early estimates by 100 per cent or more. These estimates need to be re-evaluated and refined as the project progresses to reduce the error margins. The further into a project, the 'firmer' estimates become as more information becomes available, and uncertainty is reduced; risk factors may yet unseat 'firm' estimates and these factors must be highlighted to allow project management to make appropriate contingency allowance.

It must always be accepted that later, firm estimates may change the cost/benefit reckoning to the extent that hard decisions may need to be made by the Project Board. Options may range from the omission or postponement of some system functionality to the last resort – project cancellation.

## 2.6 Who should estimate?

The responsibility for project estimating should be primarily assigned to people who have shown a capability for accurate estimating and for bringing in

## Chapter 2
## Overview of estimating

projects, whether in Project Manager or technical roles, within timescale and budget. Support for estimating in specific areas, in respect of particular risk factors, should be sought from the relevant experts. Additionally, it is often desirable to include at least one qualified estimator who is independent of the project.

There may sometimes be insufficient staff available with the appropriate skills and experience. Where there is a Project Support Office, it should be able to supply expertise in estimating. Whatever the organization, however, a conscious and planned effort should be made to build up a cadre of estimators through training and accumulating experience.

Once the estimates have been made and have been agreed by the Project Manager (or Stage/Module Manager, where different), the responsibility for delivering in line with the estimates is assumed by the Project/Stage/Module Manager.

Where IS development services are contracted out, responsibility for estimating is likely to fall to the provider, but the customer organization may wish to stipulate policies or standards for project estimating, and may wish to carry out audits or external checks for compliance with these policies and standards. It may also wish to conduct independent estimates.

Estimating responsibilities are discussed further in section 3.5.2: *People*.

# Estimating on an SSADM Project

# 3 Estimating methods

There are many estimating techniques, characterized by a number of different approaches or tactics. No specific techniques are recommended in this volume, though a sample of techniques, and their use, are given. The choice of techniques will depend on local practice within each organization.

This chapter is an introduction to estimating methods. In section 3.3 the different tactics that lie behind the various techniques are described. Section 3.4 gives some examples of estimating techniques, to illustrate the different approaches. Sections 3.3 and 3.4 include guidelines to help readers judge at what point in the project life cycle each approach and technique will be of most use. Section 3.5 describes best practices for estimating, whichever tactics and techniques are applied.

Note that contingency estimating, ie adding an allowance of effort and/or time to cover factors that cannot be accurately identified or assessed at the estimation stage, is not discussed here; it is viewed as the domain of project management rather than of any particular development methodology. Such issues should be correctly addressed within PRINCE rather than SSADM.

## 3.1 Project Model and System Model

Estimates are based, in the first place, on project characteristics and system characteristics; more formally the Project Model and System Model respectively. The Project Model is the model of how the system will be developed. The client pays for the project only in order to get the system out of it; the project itself meets no business need outside the IT organization and delivers no functionality to the user. The Project Model defines the activities to be carried out on the project and the products that are to be produced to represent the system at each stage of its development. These are what the estimators will be raising estimates for.

In SSADM terms, the Project Model is the structural model of SSADM as applied to a particular project. It defines activities in terms of the SSADM modules, stages, steps and tasks required to carry out this project. It defines project deliverables in terms of the Product

Breakdown Structure appropriate for this project. Project deliverables will also include products for project planning and control, and quality planning and control. These additional products will depend on the project management approach in place; in a PRINCE environment, for example, the overall project Product Breakdown Structure defines:

- technical products (ie the SSADM products)

- management products (eg plans, progress reports)

- quality products (eg quality review reports).

The System Model represents what will be delivered at the end of the project. The system is what the user is paying for in order to meet a business need; it delivers functionality to the user. The System Model has a defined set of inputs, outputs, procedures and data, and has a boundary that separates it from its environment.

In SSADM terms, the System Model is the model of the system as defined in the relevant SSADM Project Model via products such as Function Definitions. The final System Model is reached via transformations of the content of earlier products such as the Data Flow Model and the Logical Data Model. The System Model captures the size and complexity of the system being developed, and it is size and complexity that are the key properties of the system for estimating purposes.

SSADM projects may encompass all stages or a subset appropriate to defining a system to a level at which its progression may be referred back to the relevant decision-makers; ie a project may comprise only the stage(s) required for a Feasibility Study, or a Full Study, or just part of one – eg the Requirements Analysis module. Even a project progressed to the end of Physical Design does not deliver an implementable system that can deliver the required business functionality to the user. Thus an SSADM System Model at any defined point on a project, including the end-point of SSADM, is a snap-shot of a potential system. For estimating purposes, the System Model captures just the extent of size and complexity that belongs to the scope of the

# Chapter 3
## Estimating methods

project in terms of the planned SSADM stages. The estimating procedures below can be applied just to those parts of the life cycle required for a particular project.

**3.2 Stages**

Estimates based simply on system and project characteristics must be subject to further review, since the time and effort required for apparently very similar systems and projects can vary considerably according to environmental factors. 'Soft' environmental factors, such as people's expectations, may have a significant effect on estimates.

The overall estimating process has several distinct stages, known as the Estimating Model. These are:

**Stage 1** estimate the basic work content, ie how much effort is required to produce the system

**Stage 2** adjust the basic estimates for environmental factors

**Stage 3** schedule the work units in terms of elapsed time, taking account of dependencies between the work units (though these dependencies are not taken account of in top-down estimating – see below)

**Stage 4** determine the resources required; allocate resources to work units

**Stage 5** apply known constraints to the schedule

**Stage 6** iterate where necessary to the appropriate earlier stage.

The process and its stages, together known as the Estimating Model, are discussed further in Chapter 5. The scope of this volume is primarily Stages 1 and 2 above, as is the applicability of the approaches covered in this section.

There are a number of different approaches or tactics that can be brought together in any estimating method. Some of the approaches contrast with each other, others are complementary. Any particular technique may

# Estimating on an SSADM Project

embody several approaches, and no one approach in isolation is sufficient to define a technique. These approaches are detailed in sections 3.3.1 to 3.3.7.

## 3.3 Tactics

### 3.3.1 Top-down/bottom-up

'Top-down' and 'bottom-up' are terms with widespread currency in IT as methods of addressing problems rather than denoting any specific techniques. The top-down approach to estimating starts from a view of the project as a whole. Component parts of the project, eg major groups of activities such as project stages can, if required, be identified and seen in relation to each other or to the whole project. An example of this relationship would be the respective ratios of each project stage to the overall project size.

The bottom-up approach starts with an analysis and breakdown of the project to the lowest level required for reliable estimating. The units into which it is broken down may be task-based or product-based or both (see section 3.3.2). Estimates are attached to each unit, and these estimates are successively aggregated to higher level units such as (in SSADM) steps, stages, modules and the total project.

Both top-down and bottom-up approaches are normally followed on any project; this is recommended practice in any case, to test different estimates against each other. In general, a top-down approach is the only feasible method for a provisional estimate of the whole project early on, and can contribute to provisional estimates at any stage. The reliability of bottom-up estimates increases as the project progresses; they should always be used for firm estimates of any stage including Feasibility Study, as firm estimates are made when the detail of the stage can be identified. Top-down estimating becomes less relevant in the later stages, though stage ratios continue to be a useful check throughout.

### 3.3.2 Task-based/product-based

The task-based approach takes the basic unit for estimating as a task or activity, while the product-based approach takes project deliverables. The two approaches converge where tasks are defined in terms of delivered

Chapter 3
Estimating methods

products; this provides an objective way of identifying when a task has been completed. In this case special consideration should be given to tasks that cannot easily be associated with specific products.

The strength of each approach will depend on the characteristics of the methodology to be employed in the project being estimated. Thus task-based estimating is relevant where the methodology is well defined in terms of tasks rather than products, and product-based estimating where the methodology is well defined in terms of products rather than tasks. SSADM is well defined in both task and product terms, and so both approaches are helpful in estimating SSADM projects.

Often, task-based estimating, in terms of high-level groups of tasks such as project stages, is easier when doing initial estimates before details of the number of products and their complexity have been worked out. Product-based estimating becomes more reliable as the project advances. However, even at Feasibility Study stage, the major functional areas and entities identified can provide a basis for initial product-based estimates. In addition, a high level view of start-up events may be produced to estimate the complexity of the subsequent development work. Product-based estimating is promoted by the CCTA project management method PRINCE, which builds its plans around a Product Breakdown Structure identifying all the products of a project.

3.3.3 Algorithmic

An algorithmic approach employs a specific formula or set of formulae to calculate project estimates. The formulae operate on one or more variables relating to the system (eg entities) and apply parameters to them; typically the parameters embody environmental characteristics such as the sophistication of the development environment. Algorithmic approaches depend on the availability of historical data about projects, whether industry-wide or organization-specific.

Techniques based on an algorithmic approach may themselves work top-down or bottom-up, and be either task-based or product-based. The use of algorithmic techniques within the project life cycle will depend on

Estimating on an SSADM Project

the applicability of these other approaches to the specific situation.

3.3.4 Non-algorithmic

'Non-algorithmic' approaches range from the intuitive to the traditional bottom-up aggregation of unit estimates. The more they draw on explicit historical data, the more reliable – and probably the less intuitive – they are likely to be.

As with algorithmic approaches, non-algorithmic approaches may themselves work top-down or bottom-up, and be either task-based or product-based. Their applicability at different stages of a project thus depends on these other aspects of estimating.

3.3.5 Analogy

All estimating decisions motivated by a search for accuracy, rather than opportunism or management pressure, are made on the basis of experience. Experience may be industrial and/or organizational experience, and captured in an explicit reference database. Or the experience may be implicit, that is in people's heads, and deriving from their own experience. Algorithmic approaches employ historic reference data.

Estimating that incorporates past project experience is known as estimating by analogy, and at its simplest involves comparing the present project to one or more than one similar past project. Differences between the projects are noted and actual time expended on former projects is adjusted and used as the estimate for the new project. A more comprehensive use of analogy is the derivation and application of reference values – standard metrics to apply to tasks or products.

A key message of this volume is that experience should be recorded and thus made explicit and objective, so that decisions can be made on the basis of historical project data and of the factors that influenced the projects, rather than on the basis of fallible memory and uneven personal weightings. The availability of an explicit decision database enhances the application of each of the other approaches to estimating, be they top-down or bottom-up, task-based or product-based, algorithmic or non-algorithmic; indeed algorithmic models depend on the reference data. (Note that this is not a cheap

# Chapter 3
## Estimating methods

approach; to build up and maintain a clean and consistent set of project data requires sustained planning and effort.)

Estimating at any point in the project life cycle will benefit from reference to past projects and industry or organization standard figures. Historic information of this type is of particular benefit in early estimates, where decisions have to be made more in terms of the general characteristics of the project than of its detail; though standard figures such as stage ratios continue to be of utility throughout the project life cycle.

### 3.3.6 Expert judgement

In this case, estimates are provided by people who have had substantial experience of working on the type of activity or project being estimated. The use of expert judgement is a tactic rather than a distinct category of techniques. Each expert might be using a different technique, whether based on top-down or bottom-up, explicit or implicit analogy, algorithmic or non-algorithmic approaches. In cases where the expert approaches the problem in a top-down way, based on analogy, the use of expert judgement will be of most help in formulating initial estimates. In other cases expert judgement may be bottom-up, eg relating to a specific task or product in which the expertise lies, and may be called upon at any stage.

### 3.3.7 Tools

Previous estimates made by both analogy and expert judgement may be stored within an appropriate software tool for future reference. Many of these tools are based on expert system/knowledge based models and will allow for 'expert' generation of future estimates.

## 3.4 Techniques

Many estimating techniques are available. They range from guessing the amount of development work required to the use of complex algorithmic models. Some examples are briefly described here, with reference to the various estimating approaches that they embody. Note that automated support is available for some techniques, and should be used where possible.

### 3.4.1 Delphi technique

This technique involves consulting a number of experts, then reviewing the estimates each has made separately. It is an instance of expert judgement as discussed in

# Estimating on an SSADM Project

section 3.2, and is a procedure rather than a technique. The procedure is essentially the same as that described in Chapter 5 of this volume.

3.4.2 Traditional estimating

Traditional estimating is normally understood to refer to a bottom-up, task- or product-based, non-algorithmic technique, employing analogy to a greater or lesser extent. A guideline when using such a technique is to analyse the project down to units of 5–10 man-days.

3.4.3 Stage ratios

This technique is based on a model of a project with standard percentages for each stage, the actual values being industry- or preferably organization-specific. This means that once a particular stage has been completed, or a firm estimate agreed, estimates for the other stages can be derived by applying the ratios. This is a top-down, task-based, algorithmic technique, employing analogy through reference to an explicit decision database.

3.4.4 Function Point Analysis

This technique was originally designed for productivity assessment rather than estimating. It measures systems in terms of the functionality delivered to the user. In the version of the technique recommended by CCTA, it counts system inputs, outputs and entity references. Various weightings and environmental adjustment factors are applied. The resulting Function Point Count is the basis for estimating by the application of the particular organization's productivity figure, for example Function Points per man-month.

Function Point Analysis is a top-down technique, as it looks at the system as a whole. It is an algorithmic technique, employing analogy through the use of site standard figures for adjustment and the Function Point to effort ratio.

There is a separate Information Systems Engineering Library volume on the use of Function Point Analysis within an SSADM Version 4 project.

3.4.5 Function Weight (formerly called System Bang)

This technique counts system activities and entities, and the relationships between entities. Using these counts, it classifies the system as function-strong, data-strong or hybrid. It then applies a formula that takes into account

# Chapter 3
# Estimating methods

various types of complexity in the system under estimation, with allowance for the system classification. The resulting figure can be converted into an estimate for project effort in the same way as the Function Point Count in Function Point Analysis.

Like Function Point Analysis, Function Weight is a top-down, algorithmic technique, employing analogy.

3.4.6 Constraint models

A class of techniques is sometimes identified called constraint models. These models represent a special case of algorithmic models that allows for project constraints, eg restricted timescales or number of resources. They are thus more relevant to Stages 4 and 5 of the estimating process.

Such techniques are not necessarily, in fact, distinct techniques. Any set of project estimates, however derived, is subject to scheduling and resourcing as part of project planning. The application of constraints may lead to the revision of the estimates. For example, shortening the timescales will require extra resource, which in turn will require upwards adjustment of the unit estimates to allow for the extra communications and management effort thus entailed.

The implications of constraints can be explored non-algorithmically or algorithmically.

Constraint models can make a significant contribution to project planning for as long as there is scope to make management decisions on the basis of what the model shows. The earlier that known constraints are explored and allowed for, the more likely it is that project objectives will be achieved. Management's scope for manoeuvre diminishes as time elapses on a project, until cancellation may be the only option left! Constraint models, since they provide optimal solutions, are also useful as a cross-check on estimates and plans made by other methods.

## 3.5 Best practice

### 3.5.1 Use of approaches and techniques

The Project Manager will always wish to increase the confidence that he or she can have in the project estimates. No less important is the ability to demonstrate to management that the estimates have been prepared as thoroughly and objectively as possible. Within SSADM there are specific decision points where the inception or the continuation of a project can be reviewed. The earliest point is at the beginning of the project. Here it is still possible to draw back from committing the organization to significant expenditure; but here, also, not much project detail is likely to be available. Later on in the project re-estimates may require important decisions on project timescales and/or resourcing, or even its continuation at all.

*For these reasons, it is always advisable to employ more than one estimating approach, and more than one technique, as a cross-check.*

Significant discrepancies between estimates prepared in different ways must always be investigated; this may help in identifying areas requiring further clarification, or critical items of input data for the estimating process. Where discrepancies persist, further techniques may be employed (though the cost of maintaining expertise, records and tools across a wide range of techniques must also be considered).

The earlier in the project estimates are made, the greater the extent to which these estimates must be regarded as provisional for a high proportion of the project. This is most marked where initial commitment is made, ie before the Feasibility Study. The kind of approach that is most applicable at this point is top-down and referring to data about past projects – preferably explicit, ie by analogy, but at least implicit, eg by consulting experts.

These approaches continue to be of value when estimates are made at the end of the Feasibility Study. Here they begin to be supplemented by bottom-up estimating, as high-level functional and data models are produced. Clearly such bottom-up estimates must have wide error

# Chapter 3
## Estimating methods

ranges attached for stages other than the immediately succeeding stage.

From this point on, estimates reached via one or more of the various bottom-up techniques should be used for the next stage and where possible further stages. It is also possible, following the completion of any phase, to cross-check estimates by applying a ratio-based technique.

Detailed guidelines on the application of specific estimating approaches and techniques for SSADM are given in Chapters 6 to 8.

### 3.5.2 People

It was argued in the preceding subsection that more than one technique should be employed to prepare estimates. For similar reasons, more than one person should be asked to prepare an estimate. This provides a cross-check, and helps to get over individual bias – which may be inherent to the person, or induced by management or user pressure. (There will not be much point, however, in two runs of the same computerized algorithm, though quality checks should be carried out where there is scope for human error.)

It has been argued (Cost Estimation for Software Development: Bernard Londeix, Addison Wesley, 1987) that no-one with direct project responsibility, whether Project Manager, systems analysts or designers, should do project estimating, as they may be prone to over-optimism and subject to outside pressures. Instead, an independent Consultant Estimator should do it:

> *any professional estimator who has no direct or indirect interest in the results of the software development, except that of professional excellence.*

In practice, team members are unlikely to be excluded from estimating. They are likely to have already looked at project requirements, and the cost of their doing so will have to be borne in any case; it is also likely that they will have been selected for their relative expertise in the application and technical sides of the project. These investments are unlikely to be squandered. Nor is it necessarily advisable to do so. Each team member may have a useful insight into one or other risk area, as well as general familiarity with the proposed system. Then again, one person's optimism may well be offset by another's pessimism or tendency to 'pad' the estimates for an easier life on the project.

Team involvement in estimating is recommended not just for the reasons given above, but also because it helps to generate team commitment to meeting the estimates; the team 'buy in' to the estimates.

It remains valid, however, to require that at least one of the estimates should be made by an independent estimator, as defined above. It promotes objectivity, and at the same time gives the team estimators an extra measure of confidence and support.

For large projects, separate Stage Managers may be appointed for each stage. Where previous estimates are reviewed at the beginning of a subsequent stage, the Stage Manager will need to be involved, as he or she is required to take responsibility for delivering the stage to the estimated timescale and budget. He or she must therefore be prepared to take on this responsibility.

The qualities required by a good project estimator are *skill, judgement* and *experience*. Whatever tools are being used, there will always be variations and uncertainties to be allowed for and these need human judgement. Some estimators seem to be able to use flair and luck as a substitute for experience, knowledge, skill and plain hard work, but this is not true of the majority. Most estimators have to work hard to gain the experience to be effective. Experience should be supplemented by appropriate training.

Specific skills should include:

- professional competence in the application and technical aspects of the project (though it may not always be feasible for each estimator to have competence in all aspects)

Chapter 3
Estimating methods

- experience of working to estimates on one large project or more than one project, preferably with at least team leadership responsibility (the independent estimator should have had proven and successful project management responsibility)

- good knowledge of the development methodology being used

- understanding and experience of at least the technique he/she is applying

- ability to resist pressure from management and users

- courage where necessary to document variations in estimates imposed by management

- communication skills.

### 3.5.3 Estimating culture and environment

The accuracy of estimating will be enhanced by the adoption of some best practices to create a culture and environment conducive to good estimating.

These are considered under the general headings of:

- Use of database

- Estimating methods

- People

- Project practice.

**Use of database**

Best practice includes the following:

- establish a database of project metrics, based on defined characteristics of projects and the accumulation of the organization's or installation's experience, and drawing on industry figures where necessary

- record actual performance of completed projects and calibrate standard figures to the specific environment

# Estimating on an SSADM Project

- always keep original estimates and the assumptions and system characteristics on which they were based

- record reasons for deviation from estimates.

Note that there are proprietary database services as a complementary or alternative option to building an in-house database.

**Estimating methods**  Use the following guidelines:

- establish estimating procedures/rules that are of applicability to the organization

- select appropriate techniques for each stage in the development life cycle, both as general guidelines and taking specific project characteristics into account

- give techniques and tools time to stabilize before trying alternatives

- if using an estimating tool ensure it is calibrated with respect to the development environment.

**People**  The following good practice applies to people:

- educate managers, users and development staff with regard to the nature of estimating and the uncertainties involved (ie plus or minus a percentage confidence level)

- ensure that estimators receive the appropriate training and are involved both in the estimating and in the post-project reviewing of projects, since estimating is a skill that improves with practice.

**Project practice**  For effective estimating, follow these project practices:

- review and refine estimates at specific and standard planned points in the project and when circumstances change to render earlier assumptions unsafe

# Chapter 3
## Estimating methods

- avoid over-optimism in estimating

- identify risk factors so that project management can make appropriate decisions about contingency allowances

- carry out post-project evaluation reviews; analyse and publicize estimating lessons learnt, whether technical (methods) or political (consequences of trimming estimates to outside pressure).

Estimating on an SSADM Project

# 4 Issues affecting estimates and estimators

## 4.1 Factors to be considered in estimating

Estimates are based on:

- system characteristics – 'what will be produced'

- project characteristics – 'how it will be produced'.

These are the starting point for the approaches and techniques discussed in Chapter 3, and for the estimating procedures described in Chapters 5 to 8.

Estimates based simply on system and project characteristics must be subject to further review, since the time and effort required for apparently very similar systems and projects can vary considerably according to environmental factors. Depending on the approach and techniques employed, some of these factors may be built into the installation's calibration of estimates, as discussed in Chapter 3; others may be applied together or in isolation as judgemental factors for specific project estimates. Whichever approach is followed, these environmental factors should not be ignored. They will be revisited at the appropriate points in Chapters 5 to 8.

Although the steps within a method such as SSADM are well-defined, each project has different circumstances which will affect the timescales for the development. For example, if the project consists of experienced SSADM practitioners there will not be learning curves at the start of each new SSADM technique and the pitfalls of earlier projects will be avoided. Therefore, the estimates will be lower than for a project team approaching SSADM for the first time. In addition, the method itself may have been customized for this particular project. To accommodate these sometimes very significant differences between projects, a range of factors influencing the project must be considered, and the estimates must be adjusted accordingly. These factors which include characteristics of the project and of its environment can be categorized as organization, development team and technical.

Organizational factors:

- size of business unit affected by the system

- user awareness of IT

- IT organization's experience and status in the organization

- impact of the proposed system on the business

- organization's familiarity (both IT and user departments) with the 'type' of system being developed (ie are they going into uncharted water?)

- amount of effort to be allowed for activities such as:
  - user involvement
  - project management
  - quality assurance
  - meetings

- commitment from user management to the project, and willingness to provide adequate liaison effort

- stability of user requirements, and provision that no changes to the user requirement will be made during development, without prior re-estimation according to agreed change control procedures.

Development Team factors:

- experience level of the Project Manager

- team size (the larger the team the greater the intercommunication overhead)

- team structure (eg is a new approach such as the use of PRINCE being adopted?)

- team dynamics – are the members accustomed to working together?

# Chapter 4
## Issues affecting estimates and estimators

- experience level of development team members in:
  - the specific application
  - SSADM Version 4
  - technical resources, eg development tools.

Technical factors:

- computer type, size and complexity

- DBMS/Data Dictionary complexity

- Application Generator/4GL characteristics

- existing system software constraints

- whether the use of a new technique, such as prototyping or use of a 4GL, is planned

- availability of appropriate development tools to support analysis and design activities (particularly diagramming)

- scope for reuse of existing and proven systems or components, already developed in-house or available for purchase (ie package solution)

- security requirements

- inherent complexity of the application.

## 4.2 System and project characteristics

Besides the factors illustrated above, characteristics of the proposed system should be taken into account, such as:

- transaction rates

- performance constraints

- storage space constraints

- data structure complexity

- level of online processing required

- level of batch processing required.

# Estimating on an SSADM Project

System characteristics are considered further in Chapters 5 and 6.

Different activities will need to be performed depending upon the size and risk of the project; the selection of these activities is considered further in Chapters 5 and 6.

### 4.3 Projects database

To improve estimates it is essential to remove as much variability as possible. A database of past projects is very useful for enhancing the accuracy and reliability of this process; but the cost of generating, updating and maintaining the data must be set against these benefits. The option of making use of a commercially available database should be considered.

### 4.4 Causes of bad estimates

It cannot be repeated too often that experience is the best basis upon which to carry out estimating, and inexperience on the part of the estimator(s) can lead to unreliable estimates, whatever techniques are used and special factors allowed for. Mistakes are among the best teachers, providing that the reasons for the mistake are analysed and recorded. Mistakes in project estimating may derive from any of a number of causes. Some examples are given here.

#### 4.4.1 Lack of reliable metrics

It has been pointed out in Chapter 3 and in section 4.3 that the more metrics of past projects are retained, the more accurate will future estimates be. This does, of course, assume that the metrics collected were themselves accurate. A further qualification is that the metrics must enable comparison of like with like; there is seldom any benefit to be gained from 'stretching' metrics to a project where key characteristics are different. The effects of the lack of reliable metrics may include:

- reliance on guesswork rather than informed judgement

- vulnerability to pressure to trim estimates

- excessive time and effort spent on the estimating process.

The most damaging effects are, of course, inaccurate estimates and the likelihood of project overruns.

## Chapter 4
### Issues affecting estimates and estimators

**4.4.2 Lack of procedure**

Chapters 5 to 8 of this volume describe a set of estimating procedures. The adoption and observance of standard procedures is a necessary part of a commitment by an organization to disciplined estimating as part of project planning as a whole. The use of standard procedures means that staff may be more easily inducted into project estimating, thereby removing excessive reliance on one or two experts. Use of standard procedures assists in the planning and estimating of the estimating process itself, and ensures a more thorough set of estimates.

The lack of standard procedures may cause problems such as:

- inadequate time and care allowed for estimating, resulting in bad estimates

- excessive time spent on estimating due to *ad hoc* approaches, without necessarily providing reliable estimates

- omission of significant tasks or deliverables from the list of items estimated

- poorly or vaguely defined tasks

- failure to generate reliable metrics for future reference.

**4.4.3 Assumptions**

It is common during estimating for assumptions to be made. These assumptions may be about the characteristics of the system or the project approach to be adopted, or about the kind of organizational, development team or technical factors discussed in section 4.1 above. Invalid assumptions are a fruitful source of error, and therefore all assumptions must be documented, so that any checking of estimates by someone other than the original estimator is suitably informed; likewise revisiting assumptions and estimates in the event of subsequent changes to the specification. The availability of documented assumptions also makes it easier to conduct an 'audit trail' in the event of an investigation of the project estimates. A major benefit for estimate accuracy is that documenting an assumption forces the estimator to review the validity of the assumption being made.

Assumptions should be documented to an appropriate level of detail, to contain at least:

- what the assumption is

- why it was made and the circumstances justifying it

- dates and version identification of any documentation underlying the assumption.

### 4.4.4 Outside influence

It is by no means unknown for management to apply pressure to estimators to make their estimates fit some preconceived set of figures (eg completion by a set date). This pressure must be handled with care. There may be a case for revisiting certain estimates, for example if assumptions have been made that are within the power of management to vary. But the use of management pressure to change an estimate just in order to get different figures on paper is sheer delusion; any sets of figures can be manufactured, but delivery need not match the estimate.

Time compression is often possible at the cost of increasing the resources to be applied to the project, or dropping some of the functionality of the system. (Note that applying more resource does not necessarily enable time compression.) Phased implementation may also be an option that allows some compression of timescale.

## 4.5 Need for honesty and integrity

Estimators must be ready to explain and defend their estimates, even in cases where there can only be a very low level of confidence in the estimates; in such cases the estimators should give the reasons. A low level of confidence could mean, for example, that more work needs to be done to establish system requirements and objectives.

Estimators must have confidence in their own estimates. If they are convinced that they are the best possible, given the evidence available, they should stick with them.

# 5 Estimating procedures (general)

## 5.1 Basic procedure

The procedure in this chapter is proven and recommended good practice. It has to be acknowledged, however, that many projects cannot meet all the recommendations with the resources available to them. If only one estimator is used there is of course a greater risk of the estimate being incorrect as no check has been made on it, as was discussed in section 3.5.

This section provides a framework, the Estimating Model, and a generic set of procedures for the estimating process.

### 5.1.1 The Estimating Model

The overall estimating process has several distinct stages. These are:

1 estimate the basic work content; what system is to be produced by this project

2 adjust the basic estimates for environmental factors, such as those listed in section 4.1; note that where site-specific reference figures are used in Stage 1, some environmental factors – those common to all projects at this site – may already in effect have been allowed for, by being built into the site-specific figures

3 schedule the work units in terms of elapsed time, taking account of dependencies between the work units; this stage provides a 'logical' plan

(Note: the sequence 2 and 3 above may be reversed in some methods, but this should not affect the estimates that go forward to Stage 4.)

4 determine the resources required and allocate resources to work units; this stage provides a 'physical' plan, and the Project Manager may decide to adjust the estimates further to take account of known resource capabilities

5 apply known constraints, such as timescale required or resource limitation, to the schedule; this stage

# Estimating on an SSADM Project

may show that project objectives are at risk, and iteration through previous stages may be necessary.

The process and its stages are together known as the Estimating Model. The estimating process overlaps project planning; though at each stage of the project, estimates may need to be reviewed and revised.

The scope of this volume is primarily Stages 1 and 2 of the Estimating Model; the other stages are covered in less detail.

The procedure described below maps onto the Estimating Model as follows:

| Estimating Model | Section |
|---|---|
| Stage 1 | 5.1.2 – 5.1.5 |
| Stage 2 | 5.1.6 |
| Review (Stages 1 & 2) | 5.1.7 – 5.1.8 |
| Stages 3 to 5 | 5.1.9 |

Table 5.1: The Estimating Model

5.1.2 Initiate the estimating process

The procedures in this subsection are the responsibility of managers who are responsible for ensuring that estimating is properly carried out. They may be part of the project team, eg Project Manager, or may be independent according to local practice. In cases where the software development is contracted out, these procedures are likely to be the contractor's responsibility, but the customer organization should agree the assumptions behind the estimates, and satisfy itself of the validity of the estimates themselves.

- prepare briefing materials, to include:
  - Project Model, to current level of detail available; for example,
    - project plan
    - application products to be developed
    - product descriptions

# Chapter 5
## Estimating procedures (general)

- System Model, to current level of detail available
- indication of techniques reference material that could be consulted
- indication of relevant past project data available
- tools to be used
- assumptions to be made
- contact points for clarification of project and system detail
- plan and timescale for the estimating process

• select and brief estimators (do not give information that may influence the outcome).

5.1.3 Review the system model

The procedures in this subsection are carried out by each estimator in isolation, although they may communicate with the project team for clarification of the system requirements:

• review the System Model. This will be represented, at various successive points, by:
  - the original operational requirement (where applicable)
  - current services description
  - requirements specification
  - logical system specification
  - physical design

• clarify understanding of the system through liaison with the project team, and where required, with users via the project team

• assess the size and complexity of the required system

• assess any special factors that need to be taken into account; see section 4.1.

41

# Estimating on an SSADM Project

5.1.4 Review the Project Model

The procedures in this subsection are carried out by each estimator in isolation, although they may communicate with the project team for clarification of the project requirements:

- review the Project Model

- clarify understanding of the project approach (eg team structure, reporting and control, quality approach) through liaison with the project team where necessary

- assess the products to be produced, their scale and complexity

- where non product-specific activities (eg project management, stage reviews) are planned, assess their size and any problems likely to be encountered

- revise the basic estimating templates (examples are given in Chapter 6), to reflect the estimator's judgement concerning the products required and their significance.

5.1.5 Build the initial estimate

The procedures in this subsection are carried out by each estimator in isolation:

- review installation standard values for the various parameters (eg effort per entity or function)

- apply skill and judgement to set parameter values for this project

- apply template, or templates, to show the raw estimates for developing products at each stage and step of the method.

5.1.6 Adjust estimates for environment

The procedures in this subsection are carried out by each estimator in isolation:

- identify environmental factors relevant to the project, referring to section 4.1, any local checklists, and the estimator's own experience

Chapter 5
Estimating procedures (general)

- assess the extent to which these factors are already allowed for in installation standard values, as reviewed in section 5.1.5

- assess any special factors that need to be taken into account for this project, and adjust the estimates accordingly.

### 5.1.7 Review the adjusted estimate

The procedures in this subsection are carried out by each estimator in isolation:

- apply skill and experience to reviewing the estimates and revising any that seem excessive or light; record reasons for revisions (these may, for example, flag a particular risk area)

- reiterate this process, revisiting the Project and System Models as appropriate, until content with the estimate. The criterion should be (unless directed to some other objective at the briefing) that an appropriately qualified and experienced person could complete the defined work packages in the given environment for the effort and time estimated

- assess accuracy of the estimates and provide confidence limits if necessary.

### 5.1.8 Compare the estimates

The procedures in this subsection are carried out jointly by the various estimators:

- meet to compare estimates:
  - compare assumptions
  - review differences
  - try to resolve differences where possible

NB: care should be taken so that the strongest personality does not impose his or her estimate on the others regardless of the merit of their estimates

- where metrics are available from past projects, use them to compare the System Model and Project Model with previous cases to enhance the objectivity of the comparison process

43

Estimating on an SSADM Project

- if significant differences remain, seek further information to clarify the position

- prepare and agree new estimates as appropriate, taking care that previous estimates do not compromise the new ones; iterate from appropriate point in the procedure (section 5.1.4 will be the earliest: the estimators may well be able to agree new estimates jointly rather than produce them in isolation).

| | | |
|---|---|---|
| 5.1.9 | Resource and schedule the project | The procedures in this section are carried out by the project manager in collaboration with the estimators: |

- identify dependencies between the various work units and prepare a plan based on the work units, as so far estimated, and the dependencies

- assign resources to each work unit; consider impact of particular resource capability on the estimate for the work unit

- apply known constraints to the plan so far produced; evaluate impact on the plan, and re-iterate any preceding steps as appropriate. It may be possible, for example, to vary one or more of:
    - work content – eg omit some system facilities through discussion with the user
    - environmental factors – eg provide more powerful development aids
    - schedule of work units – eg review dependencies, look for opportunities to develop units in parallel rather than sequentially
    - resourcing – eg use more experienced people.

| | | |
|---|---|---|
| **5.2** | **Documentation and change control** | Estimates must be duly documented to site standards, and thereafter any changes to them must be kept under tight change control. |
| 5.2.1 | Document the estimates | The procedures in this subsection represent sound practice. They are the responsibility of a designated role within or independent of the project; eg Project Librarian, Project Office: |

# Chapter 5
## Estimating procedures (general)

- Date the collection of estimates, showing the names of individual estimators for future reference

- Observe local version control conventions for the housekeeping of the estimates, both the initial estimates and subsequent variations

- Identify the version of the System Model used as input to the estimating process

- Include variants on the Project Model as appropriate; variants may be due to consideration of different options

- Attach a brief statement to the finally agreed estimate indicating:
  - how it was constructed
  - the assumptions used
  - the supposed level of accuracy of the resulting estimate. It helps Project Board members if margins of error and the degree of confidence in the estimate are included. (NB: the estimate is incomplete without this statement)

- For large projects in particular, consider a further quality review of the estimates at this point.

### 5.2.2 Records of estimates

It is essential to retain, for the duration of the project, all material prepared during initial estimating and subsequent re-estimating. This is because where actual project progress records an adverse variation from estimate, there is a need to analyse the reason and attempt to take corrective action. The estimate documentation, including individual estimators' working documentation, may contain pointers to the kind of problems being encountered and the kind of corrective action to take. Particular risk or uncertainty factors, for example, may have come into play; or there may have been an implicit trade-off or even double-counting between one activity and another.

Once a project is completed, and following the post-project evaluation review, it will not be practicable or useful to keep all the records. The only reason for retention is to help to improve future estimates.

# Estimating on an SSADM Project

Retained documentation should therefore include:

- initial agreed estimates

- each subsequent set of re-estimates, with reasons for re-estimating

- assumptions made at each point, with retrospective comments on their validity

- all actuals against estimates, with reasons for any variations

- specific lessons learnt about the estimating process and the use of techniques and tools.

5.2.3 Changes to estimates

Estimates are likely to change in the course of a project. Re-estimating may be planned, or may be forced by circumstance. It should be carried out:

- at points defined in the development method; these are typically at SSADM module beginning and/or end, though not necessarily of every module – see Chapter 6

- at points required by the project management method in use; note that these points, considered as project management stages, may not correspond to those defined in the development method

- when exception conditions are identified

- when it is clear that parameter values have changed significantly and that a higher degree of confidence can be placed in the new values

- when significant new products, or changes to planned products, are identified, and these changes to scope have been discussed at the appropriate level.

Each re-estimate should briefly identify the reason for re-estimating and the changes in the basis for estimating, eg in assumptions or the System Model, since the last estimate. Note that re-estimates should always be

# Chapter 5
## Estimating procedures (general)

formulated and recorded as the value for a whole task being re-estimated, even when work on it has already begun, rather than just for the work believed to remain outstanding on it.

### 5.3 Project, module and stage estimating

The models (system, project and estimating) and the procedure described in section 5.1 apply to each level of estimating, whether for the project as a whole or for parts of it, such as SSADM modules or development stages. These may correspond to a greater or lesser extent with project management stages (see section 5.2.3). In this section some considerations about the differences between and interrelationships among these levels are discussed; 'stage' here means project management stage, as for example in PRINCE.

Initial estimates that are used to formulate the Project Plan are the most difficult to create since there are so many uncertainties and unknowns at the time they are drawn up. As discussed in Chapter 3, top-down estimating and estimating by analogy is likely to have been influential at this stage. A high variance between the initial and the final estimate is probable.

Plans for each project management stage must be produced, with firm estimates. Stage planning is the next level of detail beneath the Project Plan level. More confidence can be placed in the parameter values here than at initial project planning level, as the estimator is working at a more detailed level and estimating is based on bottom-up approaches.

Estimates made for stage plans are likely to be subject to influence from the provisional estimates made earlier in the Project Plans for the stage; indeed it is almost unavoidable. Two factors can help to counteract this:

- involvement of some estimators who are unaware of what the higher level plans indicate

- increasing reliance on bottom-up rather than top-down estimating.

Estimates made at each point in the project, whether the initial, provisional estimates or later firm ones, are used to prepare schedules based on the estimated activity durations, with upper and lower variations. Dependencies are defined and resourcing decisions made. The resulting plan is tested against any known constraints, possibly leading to replanning and/or reviews of estimates. Here again, care should be taken to preserve some degree of separation between project and stage planning.

The accuracy of the estimating and re-estimating process, and implications of estimating at different levels during a project, should be reviewed for each project. This should form part of the post-project evaluation review of the project.

## 5.4 Software support

The efficiency and accuracy of estimating, and the record keeping of the resulting estimates, are likely to be much enhanced through the support of an appropriate software system. Here, as in many other cases, there is a choice of 'make or buy'. The options are discussed in this section, and guidance on both the make and the buy routes is given.

### In-house solution

Unless the systems they develop are almost unique in nature, organizations are very unlikely to find it economic to develop an estimating system from scratch. Estimating workbenches are available for the price of a couple of days' work. The approach recommended if a decision to buy a proprietary product is not forthcoming is to employ a spreadsheet; there will almost certainly be one or more of them around the office.

The estimating templates are loaded into the spreadsheet and used to facilitate the process of estimating, re-estimating and record keeping. An example of such a spreadsheet solution is given in Annex C.

### Estimating workbenches

Criteria for the selection of an estimating workbench should be defined to take account of any particular needs of the organization. These should include the organization's general criteria, common to any such procurement; for example, usability, supplier stability and the quality of support offered.

# Chapter 5
## Estimating procedures (general)

The fundamental criterion for selection of an estimating workbench is suitability for the environment in which it is to support project estimating; in particular, the ability to model the system development method(s) in place, and to employ installation-specific reference figures.

Within the above criterion, there are a number of more detailed selection criteria specific to the estimating systems chosen:

- the ability to calibrate and recalibrate the workbench

- the ability to generate and compare several versions of an estimate prior to installing the most realistic one

- the ability to derive the basic metrics from system products generated through the use of a CASE tool; these products can be extracted from the CASE dictionary for the relevant stage or step of SSADM

- the ability to compare earlier estimates of a stage or step with ones based on more recent metrics

- multi-project capability and the ability to store and compare estimates from different projects

- the ability to trace how particular estimates are derived

- the ability to export estimates into a project planning tool

- the ability to configure the basic parameters and the database underlying the method

- storage of actuals (preferably imported from project planning and control tool) and comparisons with estimates

- the ability to include descriptions as well as just numbers to identify the various tasks and products

- ease of modelling the estimates at the various levels of the Project Model (eg step, stage, module)

## Estimating on an SSADM Project

- the ability to include both product-based and task-based estimates

- the number of tasks and products the workbench can cater for

- production of printed reports and documentation about the estimates.

Note that whichever workbench is selected, it is vital that it should be calibrated to the specific environment; variations in installation productivity of upwards of 1:3 are not uncommon. Recalibration must also be undertaken regularly to take account of changes in the environment, such as skill level and CASE support.

# 6 Developing estimates for SSADM projects

**6.1 Introduction to suggested procedure**

The approach suggested in this chapter is applicable at any level of estimating: project, module or detailed. The approach is suitable for use initially with minimal sizing data so that it can be applied from the earliest point possible in the lifecycle. The approach can be carried out manually, but it is strongly recommended that automated support – a spreadsheet at the very least – should be used, as discussed in section 5.4.

The approach is relevant whether a workbench, spreadsheet, or just paper and calculator are being used. Clearly a workbench may impose certain constraints in terms of the source data for estimating, but most such products have enough flexibility to allow estimating based on the kind of data discussed in this chapter; supplemented where desired by existing in-house estimating practices. The example given in Annex C, building on the procedures described in section 6.3, is based on the use of a spreadsheet. This is not intended as a physical specification of a recommended system, but rather as a statement of the logical data required.

This method of working provides practitioners with the opportunity to use a consistent approach and to learn from experience. The approach will help to ensure that everything of relevance is considered, especially at or near the beginning of a project, when estimates are generated from minimal data.

It is particularly important that a correct and thorough approach is adopted right from the start of an IS project since estimates set then can acquire a significance that is hard to dispute, even when more precise data have been gathered.

In section 6.4 specific estimating points in the lifecycle are identified, and their characteristics described, in terms of the balance of certainty and uncertainty attaching to estimates at these points. This balance helps to identify the type of technique to use at each point.

## Estimating on an SSADM Project

**6.2 Project activities and considerations**

The method of estimating described in this chapter is based on SSADM Version 4 products and activities but consideration must also be given to other activities. Some of these were mentioned in Chapter 4. They are activities that must be carried out on any project, but may not be related to any specific product, or explicitly prescribed in the methodology. They include:

- user liaison:
  - analyst's time with the users – eg for interviews and their respective write-ups
  - user effort required, where estimates are supposed to include this effort.

(Note that estimates should be appropriately weighted to allow for the involvement of multiple user areas and for geographical distribution.)

- quality review (both formal, ie Project Assurance Team, and peer group review):
  - circulation of material for review
  - reviewers' preparation
  - review meeting
  - follow-up actions.

- project support:
  - continuity of project development activities through the Project Support Office or the Project Assurance Team
  - administrative control against schedules and budgets
  - user assurance control and representation
  - other support services for the project.

- management considerations:
  - people management
  - technical management
  - project planning and control
  - meetings of the Project Board, user management and others.

**6.3 Principles and procedures**

The principles and procedures in this section are intended to complement the 'Basic Procedure' described in section 5.1, with aspects specific to SSADM.

# Chapter 6
## Developing estimates for SSADM projects

### 6.3.1 System Model

Some basis for estimating the complexity and size of the problem, and other relevant system attributes, must be available from the start. This could be a statement of requirements presented in SSADM terms, albeit at a very high level, initially at least.

Once a project is fully under way, detailed information from the System Model should be substituted for any assumptions used initially. Initial tailoring of SSADM may have been carried out during early development, but this should always be documented with the related risks and the compromises made.

Some example attributes derived from the System Model are:

- number of processes on data flow diagrams

- number of I/O Data Flows

- number of entities on logical data structure

- number of Attributes/Data Items

- number of requirements.

### 6.3.2 Project Model

Planning can be carried out at four levels: Project, Module, Stage and Step. SSADM Version 4 is structured into modules as the mandatory planning units. The project management approach adopted will determine what project management planning stages will be defined; these will not necessarily coincide with SSADM stages, but should at least coincide with module boundaries.

At the project planning level the full SSADM structural model should be used. Module planning will use an expanded version of the SSADM structural model for the module in question (ie extra products and activities will be shown as appropriate). Detailed planning at the step level will use an expanded version of the SSADM structural model for the stage in question.

### 6.3.3 Estimating parameters

The Project Model defines a number of deliverables or products. These are represented in the Product Breakdown Structure for the project. In reviewing the Project Model, the estimators may add further products to the model.

Some products will be singular in nature (eg the Prototyping Report, the Logical Datastore/Entity Cross-Reference of the Current Services LDM), but most have a structure of components (eg the Entity and Relationship Descriptions in the Current Environment and the Required System Logical Data Model).

The estimators' task is to examine the System Model available to them and determine the values appropriate for each parameter. On the first attempt, only the original values should be entered. Thereafter, the estimators' original values are preserved and revised values are used; the estimator should number and preserve each attempt. As the project progresses, the majority of the revised values should be derived directly from the present state of the System Model at the time of estimating. This will give an increasingly accurate guide to estimating as the project progresses.

Early estimates will require the estimator to make judgements about the probable values.

### 6.3.4 Estimating template

Chapter 7 and Annex C provide an example of a template for estimating SSADM projects. The template always has two parts:

- the Parameter List
- the Project Model.

It is the estimator's responsibility to determine the relevant parameters for the Parameter List derived from the appropriate System Model and to determine the products and activities set out in the Project Model. It must be emphasized that this volume only presents guidance on the approach to be used in estimating for SSADM projects, together with the illustrative example in Chapter 7 and Annex C.

# Chapter 6
## Developing estimates for SSADM projects

The example, in particular the figures used, must not be used as it stands without critical reappraisal by the estimators. This is particularly true at the detailed planning level, eg Step 150 may involve very little work in some cases and a great deal in others. Only those working on the project will be aware of the level of work required and be able to take account of such differences.

### 6.4 When to estimate in SSADM Version 4

Annex A identifies the points in the SSADM structural model where estimating should be carried out. These points are where estimating and re-estimating should be scheduled into the project plan; clearly, re-estimating may also be triggered by exception conditions on the project in between scheduled estimating points. At some of these points, the estimates being made are provisional in nature; at others, firm estimates are being made.

In some cases both firm estimates for the next module and provisional estimates for the remaining modules are required. (It must always be remembered that there is a spectrum from provisional to firm; the distinction is not a black and white one. The uncertainty attached to provisional estimates should diminish as the project progresses and more information about the system is available, until at estimating points H and I the provisional and firm estimates will be based on the same information and be of more or less equal reliability.)

Annex B shows, for each estimating point:

- whether a provisional or firm estimate is being made (both, in some cases)

- the SSADM modules covered by each estimate

- an indication of the kinds of information that are known about the System and Project Models at each point, and the kind of unknown that may introduce uncertainty into the estimate

- the type of approach or tactic that is applicable, in the terms described in Chapter 3

- examples of techniques and approaches within the types of approach identified.

# Estimating on an SSADM Project

# 7 Estimating SSADM Version 4 projects using a spreadsheet

## 7.1 Introduction

This chapter describes how to use an estimating method based on the approach described in Chapter 6 and using the spreadsheet provided in Annex C. This spreadsheet uses a number of system components (eg entities), a project complexity factor and a project adjustment factor to produce estimates for each SSADM step. The spreadsheet will give estimates for Stages 1 to 5 of SSADM Version 4. Stage 6 has not been included as the work carried out is so dependent on the technical environment chosen that it is not helpful to produce generalized estimates.

The spreadsheet assumes the use of a typical CASE tool. Estimates need to be adjusted downwards if a more sophisticated tool, that is one which carries out transformations automatically, is used. For example if the tool were capable of producing skeleton ECDs from ELHs the estimates for Step 360 would be lower.

It is recommended that this spreadsheet is used together with the Function Point Analysis (FPA) spreadsheet, in Annex D, so that results from each can be cross-checked. For a detailed description of how to use the FPA spreadsheet see Chapter 8.

## 7.2 Using the spreadsheet

There are four components to the estimating method:

- creation of initial parameters, estimates of the number of components such as interviews, DFDs, entities, etc, and estimates of project characteristics, such as percentage of the system that is on-line

- calculation of a system complexity factor

- calculation of the project adjustment factor, to take some account of environment, management structure, team composition, etc

- using the estimating spreadsheet, to give an estimate in man-days for each SSADM workstep.

Estimating on an SSADM Project

It is assumed that there is sufficient information in the Project Initiation Document to define the initial set of estimating parameters described in section 7.4. If not, the project manager must make estimates of the initial values.

NB. The formulae used for estimating are very general, and, in the absence of more precise guidance will give man-day estimates that are reasonable for a model SSADM project, ie a project where there is a reasonable balance between complexity of data and complexity of function, between update processing and enquiries, etc. However, many projects will differ from this assumed model, and the more a project deviates from the model, the less reasonable the standard estimates will be. The most effective way to use the spreadsheet is to collect actual figures from projects, compare them with estimates, and update the formulae to reflect experience. This way the spreadsheet will gradually become more reliable within the organization.

7.3 **Input from the Project Initiation Document**

The following items are required and may be quickly developed or estimated from the Project Initiation Document :

- identification of key user areas (typically between 1 and 4 )

- overview DFD showing major functional areas and interfaces (typically between 1 and 6 major functions)

- overview LDM for each key user area

- estimate of the number of major documents and transactions in the system.

7.4 **Initial parameters**

7.4.1 Define initial parameters

The initial parameters required for estimating complexity, adjustment and man-days are:

- **Major system processes** – the number of major business functions/processes on the exploratory DFD, usually between 1 and 6

58

# Chapter 7
## Estimating SSADM Version 4 projects using a spreadsheet

- **User areas affected by system** – usually between 1 and 4

- **User view entities** – the number of different entities across all the exploratory LDMs for the user areas (usually between 10 and 15)

- **Key interviews** – agree with the users on who should be the subjects of in-depth key interviews in each user area (usually one manager and one or two operational staff)

- **Major reports** – estimate the number of major reports in the system (usually between 5 and 30).

7.4.2 Determine project characteristics

The spreadsheet has default values set for project characteristics, but wherever possible these defaults should be overwritten with project-specific values. The following project characteristics are used together with the initial parameters described in section 7.4.1 to produce the derived parameters and thus estimates of man-days:

- **Percentage of new requirements** – an estimate of the percentage of the system that is made up of new requirements. Clearly the ratio between new requirements and current services has an impact on the estimates. The default used for 'percentage of new requirements' is 50 per cent

- **Percentage on-line** – an estimate of the percentage of the new system that is to be on-line. The default used for 'percentage on-line' is 50 per cent

- **Percentage enquiry functions** – an estimate of the percentage of the new system functions that are expected to be wholly enquiry. The default used for 'percentage enquiry functions' is 30 per cent

- **Percentage of dialogues to be prototyped** – an estimate of the percentage of the dialogues that are to be prototyped. The default used for 'percentage of dialogues to be prototyped' is 50 per cent

# Estimating on an SSADM Project

- **Percentage of reports to be prototyped** – an estimate of the percentage of the major reports that are to be prototyped. The default used for 'percentage of reports to be prototyped' is 50 per cent

- **Number of BSOs** – the expected number of Business System Options to be developed. The default used for 'number of BSOs' is 3

- **Number of TSOs** – the expected number of Technical System Options to be developed. The default used for 'number of TSOs' is 3.

### 7.4.3 Validation

The initial parameters should be reviewed for reasonable size and level of detail.

In particular, the number of functional areas on the exploratory DFD should be given careful thought, since many of the other parameters are based on it. The size of functional area envisaged is a self-contained business area (not necessarily restricted to only one group of users), or current computer subsystem.

If the exploratory DFD has been taken to too great a level of detail, the estimates will be inflated unrealistically.

## 7.5 Project complexity

On the estimating spreadsheet, there are three standard man-day rates for each estimating parameter. These three man-day rates relate to the complexity of the project. Type 1 projects are the least complex, Type 2 are moderately complex and Type 3 are the most complex. The project complexity factor is input on page 1 of the spreadsheet. To derive the project complexity follow the procedure below:

1 Give the project an initial score of 18 points

2 Estimate each of the system characteristics listed in Table 7.1. For each, depending on the value estimated, subtract, ignore or add the listed weight to the project score, as indicated in the table

## Chapter 7
### Estimating SSADM Version 4 projects using a spreadsheet

3   The project will finish with a score between 0 and 36. Assign it a complexity rating, Type 1, Type 2 or Type 3, as indicated at the foot of the table.

The complexity factor is normally applied to the whole system. Sometimes, in working through the table, you may decide that a step of the particular project is significantly more or less complex than the rest of the project. In such cases, use the 'step complexity' column on the estimating spreadsheet.

| System characteristic | | Subtract | Ignore | Add | Weight |
|---|---|---|---|---|---|
| Inputs | - batch | 1 – 20 | 21 – 50 | > 50 | 1 |
| | - online | 1 – 10 | 11 – 50 | > 50 | 1 |
| Outputs | - major reports | 1 – 30 | 31 – 60 | > 60 | 1 |
| | - minor reports | 1 – 30 | 31 – 60 | > 60 | 1 |
| | - online enquiries | 1 – 20 | 21 – 50 | > 50 | 1 |
| Data elements | | < 100 | 100 – 500 | > 500 | 2 |
| Complex computations | | < 50 | 50 – 100 | > 100 | 2 |
| Required online response | | > 10 sec | 2 – 9 sec | < 2 sec | 2 |
| Interfaces with other applications | | few, uni-directional | few, bi-directional, non-critical | many, bi-directional, critical | 4 |
| Impact of system on organization | | minor | major | critical | 3 |

| Project complexity | Score |
|---|---|
| Type 1 | 0 – 10 |
| Type 2 | 11 – 25 |
| Type 3 | 26 – 36 |

Table 7.1: Project complexity factor

61

## Estimating on an SSADM Project

| Contributing factor | Size or scope | % effect |
|---|---|---|
| *Organization* | | |
| Number of user areas involved in system | 1 | 95% |
| | 2 | N/E |
| | > 2 | 105% |
| Size of user division affected | up to 50 staff | 95% |
| | 50 – 500 staff | N/E |
| | > 500 staff | 105% |
| User familiarity with application | extensive | 95% |
| | moderate | N/E |
| | minimal (eg new business) | 105% |
| User decision makers | key individual | 95% |
| | single committee with key individuals | N/E |
| | multiple committees, multiple reviews | 105% |
| ADP structure in organization | single decision maker | 90% |
| | established hierarchy, strong project management | N/E |
| | complex organization, multiple decision makers | 110% |
| *Team Composition* | | |
| Project Team structure | 3 or fewer in team, 1 decision maker | 90% |
| | 4 – 8 in team, external technical approval | N/E |
| | > 8 in team, multiple decision makers | 110% |
| Experience with application | extensive, or consultant available | 95% |
| | considerable | N/E |
| | none | 105% |
| *Technical Experience* | | |
| General | all experienced analysts and designers | 95% |
| | balance of experienced staff and newly trained | N/E |
| | experienced leader with a newly trained team | 105% |
| Dictionary & DBMS | extensive experience | 95% |
| | previously used by some of the team | N/E |
| | new to team | 105% |
| Methodology | extensive experience | 90% |
| | at least 1 experienced team member | N/E |
| | new to team | 115% |

Table 7.2: Project adjustment factor

# Chapter 7
## Estimating SSADM Version 4 projects using a spreadsheet

**7.6 Project adjustment factor**

The project adjustment factor is a percentage used in all stages to adjust the man-days, and is input on Page 1 of the estimating spreadsheet.

To derive the project adjustment factor give the project an initial score of 100, then multiply by the percentages as indicated in Table 7.2. ('N/E' means 'no effect'.)

It is theoretically possible to derive an adjustment factor of more than 195 per cent. However, if the adjustment factor is greater than about 140 per cent, the project is potentially at risk. Consider whether it is wise to start the project as it is currently planned, or whether, for example, a more experienced team, a smaller project and simpler decision-making procedures would be safer.

**7.7 Spreadsheet**

**7.7.1 Spreadsheet structure**

The spreadsheet has two parts:

- a header page, on which initial parameters and project characteristics (derived from the Project Initiation Document) are entered, together with the project complexity and adjustment factors

- pages for each module of SSADM, with a section for each workstep.

If you have an organization-standard spreadsheet make a copy, giving it a name appropriate to your project, or construct your own using the supplied parameters.

**7.7.2 Estimating parameters**

On page 1 of the spreadsheet, fill in initial estimates for the first five Project Initiation Document parameters (as described in section 7.4):

- *major system processes*

- *user areas*

- *user view entities*

- *key interviews*

- *major reports*.

# Estimating on an SSADM Project

Enter values, if they can be determined, for each of the following project characteristics:

- *percentage new requirements*
- *percentage on-line*
- *percentage enquiry functions*
- *percentage of dialogues to be prototyped*
- *percentage of reports to be prototyped*
- *number of BSOs*
- *number of TSOs.*

Default values should be used for these parameters if values cannot be derived from the information in the Project Initiation Document. However, estimates will be less dependable if project specific values are not entered.

Initial (default) estimates for the next 14 parameters are automatically derived as follows:

- *support interviews* – key interviews x 2
- *level 2 DFDs* – major system processes x 2
- *new functions* – level 2 DFDs x 5 x percentage new requirements
- *functions in required DFD* – level 2 DFDs x 5
- *key functions* – required functions x 0.3
- *LDM entities* – user view entities x 3
- *ELH events* – entities x 3.5
- *TNF sources* – required functions x 1.5
- *required system LDM entities* – entities x 1.333
- *TNF submodels* – TNF sources ÷ 6

# Chapter 7
## Estimating SSADM Version 4 projects using a spreadsheet

- *enquiries* – required functions x percentage enquiry functions

- *dialogues* – required functions x percentage online

- *key reports* – major reports x percentage of reports to be prototyped

- *key dialogues* – dialogues x percentage of dialogues to be prototyped.

These values are likely to be of the right sort of order, but are unlikely all to be reasonable for any given project. Review each of them, and where appropriate overwrite them with more realistic values, based on experience and knowledge of the project and the application.

Enter the project adjustment factor as a percentage, and enter the project complexity as 1 (Type 1), 2 (Type 2) or 3 (Type 3).

### 7.7.3 Stage and workstep estimates

In the main body of the spreadsheet, man-day estimates will be generated for each workstep within each stage. These estimates will be based on the Project Initiation Document and derived parameters input and calculated on page 1 of the spreadsheet.

For each estimating parameter (*Est Unit*) applicable to a workstep there will be an entry for:

- **Units** Number of entities, interviews etc, based on the initial estimates for the first five Project Initiation Document parameters input on page 1 of the spreadsheet

- **Step Cmpx** Step complexity factor. Normally the project complexity factor (1, 2 or 3) input on page 1 of the spreadsheet, but can be different if that particular step is more or less complex than the rest of the project. If, for example, a project is moderate (Type 2), but a few of the worksteps are expected to be disproportionately complex, change the complexity to 3 for those worksteps

65

- **Days/Unit** One of the three standard man-day rates for that estimating parameter. The man-day rate is selected from the *Unit Days* column that relates to the step complexity factor

- **Std Days** Standard man-day estimate = days/unit x units

- **Adjstd Days** Adjusted man-day estimate, taking account of project environment, management structure, team composition etc, = std days x project adjustment factor, rounded up to nearest man-day.

The adjusted man-day estimates for each estimating parameter are aggregated to give a subtotal for each step. Similarly, step subtotals are aggregated to give a total man-day estimate for each stage.

The work can then be apportioned between the skill and responsibility profiles of the personnel on the project team, as a first step towards work packaging.

### 7.7.4 Fitting the estimates to the project

The estimating criteria underpinning the method just described are based on a 'standard' SSADM project and any actual project will differ from the standard in some ways.

The estimating criteria tend towards cautious and generous estimates. Usually, the effect of differences between the actual project and the assumed standard is to inflate the estimates. They should be reviewed to see if any can be reduced.

After the estimates have been produced on the spreadsheet, go through each item and review whether the expected number of components and the amount of time to develop them is reasonable in view of the particular project circumstances. Concentrate first on those items that have the largest numbers of man-days. Remember when reviewing that the estimates include time for documentation and quality assurance for the authors of end products, but not for others, such as users or an inspection team from outside the project.

## Chapter 7
### Estimating SSADM Version 4 projects using a spreadsheet

Where estimates are altered, document the reasons for alteration in the project log and pay particular attention to actual time (including quality assurance) in the project control system.

7.7.5 Updating the estimates

Parameters for later steps are defined in terms of those used for earlier steps. As the project progresses, actual values will be obtained for parameters. These are used in two ways:

- revised estimates can be produced, based on the actual values, for any subsequent parameters that are defined in terms of them

- the actual values are fed back into standards, to improve the guidelines and formulae in the estimating method package.

Estimating on an SSADM Project

# 8 Estimating SSADM projects using the Mk II Function Point Analysis spreadsheet

## 8.1 Introduction

This chapter describes how to use the spreadsheet in Annex D to support the use of Mk II Function Point Analysis when estimating an SSADM Version 4 project. For full details of estimating SSADM projects using Mk II Function Point Analysis, see the Information Systems Engineering (ISE) Library volume: *Estimating with Mk II Function Point Analysis*.

The formulae used in the spreadsheet are those taken from that volume. These formulae are based on empirical observations and on industry average environments. To give reliable results the estimating formulae should be calibrated for the target environment. The ISE Library volume gives advice on this calibration.

It is recommend that this spreadsheet is used together with the estimating spreadsheet in Annex C, so that results from each can be cross-checked.

Note that throughout this chapter the person using the spreadsheet is referred to as the 'estimator'. The term 'user' is reserved for the eventual user of the computer system.

## 8.2 Overview of the Mk II Function Point estimating method

Mk II Function Point Analysis (FPA) is a top-down estimating technique that uses global characteristics of the system to produce the estimates.

The aim of the technique is to estimate the elapsed time it is expected to take to produce a deliverable and the cost of producing it. The cost only addresses the cost of human resources in work hours. Estimators must consider other costs, eg hardware, separately. The technique is for use on transaction based application systems, which manipulate data stored in files or databases.

The size of the system is estimated in Mk II function points using the size of the information processing logic and a technical complexity adjustment factor. The information processing logic size is measured by analysing the logical transactions that make up a system. In SSADM terms a logical transaction is the processing of an event or an enquiry. The technical complexity adjustment is determined by considering the degree of influence of nineteen or more technical characteristics of the system. The total system size is then calculated by multiplying the information processing logic size by the technical complexity adjustment.

The adjusted system size is used to produce a normative estimate of the total effort and elapsed time required to develop the system. The effort and elapsed time are distributed across the modules/phases of the project. The effect of project specific characteristics that may influence the developers' performance are taken into account in the estimates as are any deadlines that have been imposed on the project.

The full-time equivalent headcount required for each module/phase is calculated. The estimator rounds the headcount figures and adjusts them to match the availability of personnel.

At several steps within the FPA method, industry average weightings or coefficients are used. In the organization's first projects to be estimated using Mk II FPA these industry average figures should be used. However, as typical projects are completed, data should be collected for use later in calibrating the estimating method. The weights and coefficients that may be calibrated are:

- the Mk II FPA weights used in Stage 1, Step 2 – advice on calibration is given in Section 7.7 of the ISE Library volume

- the technical complexity adjustment co-efficient used in Stage 1, Step 4 – advice on calibration is given in Section 7.8 of the ISE Library volume

- the system size/productivity relationship used in Stage 2, Step 1 – advice on calibration is given in Chapter 6 of the ISE Library volume

# Chapter 8
## Estimating SSADM projects using the Mk II Function Point Analysis spreadsheet

- the system size-delivery relationship used in Stage 2, Step 3 – advice on calibration is given in Chapter 6 of the ISE Library volume

- the effort and schedule percentage profiles by module or phase used in Stage 3

- the effect on performance of the risk factors used in Stage 4.

Great care should be taken when calibrating the size-productivity relationship and the size/delivery relationship.

### 8.3 Assembling the inputs for the FPA spreadsheet

Listed below are the minimum input requirements for Mk II FPA:

- a logical data model

- a description of the system functions, both update and enquiry, and an indication of whether they are online or batch

- an assessment of the technical characteristics of the system, eg high transaction rates

- an assessment of the implementation environment, eg use of 4GL or 3GL

- an installation style guide that sets the general standards that should be adhered to for any systems development.

The first three of these inputs are available in a completed form towards the end of the Requirements Specification module (the end of Stage 3). The last two inputs will not be available in a completed form until the end of Stage 4, Technical System Options (TSOs). This would indicate that accurate estimates can only be produced at the end of Requirements Specification or even at the end of TSOs.

However, planning and estimating should be a process of continual assessment, re-estimating and replanning in response to more detailed information becoming

Estimating on an SSADM Project

available. Even at the end of the Feasibility Study it should be possible to make some assessment of each of the above inputs to produce initial estimates. As analysis and design progresses more detailed information about the system is discovered and the estimates can be refined.

Below is a summary, for each of the first three SSADM Modules, of the SSADM products that may be input to FPA. The estimator should consider re-estimating the project at each of these points:

- Feasibility Study

- Requirements Analysis

- Requirements Specification (after Steps 310 and 320)

- Requirements Specification (at the end of the module).

### 8.3.1 Feasibility Study

During the Feasibility Study it will be possible to make an assessment of system size using the SSADM documentation available and by applying some rules of thumb to classify logical transactions. An assessment of system size can be made for each Feasibility Option, which may aid the selection process, in which case it would be reasonable only to assess the size of the selected option if it were a hybrid of two or more options or if confirmation of the original sizing was required.

The following SSADM products should be consulted at this point:

- Context Diagram to provide an overview of the proposed system

- Data Flow Diagrams (DFDs) and, if they exist, supporting Elementary Process Descriptions, to identify the major functions and the events processed within those functions and hence the logical transactions

# Chapter 8
## Estimating SSADM projects using the Mk II Function Point Analysis spreadsheet

- Overview Logical Data Structure and, if they exist, Entity Descriptions to ensure that logical transactions have been identified to create, update and possibly delete the primary entities

- Requirements Catalogue to confirm that all update logical transactions have been identified from the DFDs and to identify enquiry functions, which usually do not appear on the DFDs, for inclusion in the logical transactions

- Outline Required Environment Description contained in the Feasibility Report to assess the technical characteristics of the system.

Although a reasonable estimate of the logical transactions can be made at this point, there will not be a detailed description of the inputs to, the outputs from, or the entities referenced by these transactions. The ISE Library volume advises that the transactions identified may be classified as simple, average or complex and from this classification estimates can be made of the numbers of input attributes, output attributes and entities referenced. See Figure 11 in section 7.2 of the volume. Another approach is to compare the transactions in the proposed system with those in a similar existing system and use figures from the existing system.

If IS Strategy Planning is in place in your organization, it may be useful to refer to the Management and Technical Policies and the Technical Framework document for information on the technical environment for the proposed system. If an SSADM Feasibility Study is not to be carried out these outputs from the strategic planning will provide useful input to FPA at the end of Requirements Analysis and Requirements Specification.

### 8.3.2 Requirements Analysis

By the end of the Requirements Analysis module the system functionality will be defined in greater detail, in the Data Flow Model (DFM) and the Requirements Catalogue, allowing a more accurate assessment of logical transactions to be made. The DFM will also have I/O Descriptions, enabling the first real evaluation of input and output attributes and entity references.

Estimating on an SSADM Project

The following products should be consulted at this point:

- Logical Data Flow Model, especially DFDs, Elementary Process Descriptions and I/O Descriptions to identify current system logical transactions, input and output attributes and entity types referenced

- Logical Data Store/Entity Cross-reference to identify the entity types referenced by logical transactions that appear on the DFDs

- Logical Data Model, especially the Entity Descriptions to validate the identification of logical transactions and to assist in the identification of entity types referenced

- Requirements Catalogue to extend the logical transactions identified to include enquiries and the additional update requirements of the new system, both of which at this point are only documented in the Requirements Catalogue

- Feasibility Report and/or the outputs from strategic planning to assess the technical characteristics of the system

- the selected Business System Option.

Where the Business System Options vary significantly in scope or content there may be a case for planning separately for each option as an aid to the selection process. The subsequent selected option will almost inevitably be an amalgam of two or more of the options put to the project board; therefore, a further assessment should be made of the selected option.

8.3.3 Requirements Specification (after Steps 310/320)

It may be worthwhile rechecking estimates after Steps 310 and 320 have been carried out. At this point the new requirements for the system will have been documented in detail for the first time in the Data Flow Model and Logical Data Model making it easier to identify the logical transactions.

# Chapter 8
## Estimating SSADM projects using the Mk II Function Point Analysis spreadsheet

The following products should be consulted at this point:

- Required Data Flow Model, especially DFDs, Elementary Process Descriptions and I/O Descriptions to identify required system logical transactions, input and output attributes and entity types referenced

- Logical Data Store/Entity Cross-reference to identify the entity types referenced by logical transactions that appear on the DFDs

- Logical Data Model, especially the Entity Descriptions, to validate the identification of logical transactions and to assist in the identification of entity types referenced

- Requirements Catalogue to extend the logical transactions identified to include enquiries that are only documented in the Requirements Catalogue at this point

- Feasibility Report and/or the outputs from strategic planning to assess the technical characteristics of the system.

8.3.4 Requirements Specification (at the end of the module)

By the end of the Requirements Specification module the system processing will be clearly defined by the Function Definitions, Effect Correspondence Diagrams (ECDs) and Enquiry Access Paths (EAPs) so that an accurate assessment of system size is possible. Entity types referenced by events and enquiries are clearly documented in ECDs and EAPs. Input and output attributes are clearly defined in I/O Structures.

The following products should be consulted at this point:

- Function Definitions to identify the logical transactions, both update and enquiry

- I/O Structures to identify the input and output attributes for the logical transactions

75

Estimating on an SSADM Project

- Effect Correspondence Diagrams to identify the entity types referenced by events (logical transactions)

- Enquiry Access Paths to identify the entity types referenced by enquiries (logical transactions)

- Feasibility Report and/or the outputs from strategic planning to assess the technical characteristics of the system.

Note that the Event/Entity Matrix may be an aid in identifying entity types referenced by an event, but this product is not always maintained. The same information can be gleaned from the ECDs and EAPs. The Data Flow Model may be used to validate the information derived from the Function Definitions and I/O Structures.

If any work is carried out on Technical System Options before the end of Stage 3 then any relevant information concerning the technical characteristics of the system should be fed into the FPA estimating process.

## 8.4 Step by step guide to the FPA spreadsheet

The Function Point Analysis (FPA) spreadsheet follows the steps in Chapter 5, *A step by step guide to the estimating method*, of the ISE Library volume.

To get started, if you have an organization-standard FPA Estimating spreadsheet make a copy, giving it a name appropriate to your project, or construct your own using the supplied parameters.

### 8.4.1 Stage 1 – Assess the system size in Mk II function points

**Step 1– Enter the total attribute and entity parameters**
The estimator enters the total number over all logical transactions of:

- input attribute types

- entity types referenced

- output attribute types.

Separate totals must be input for the on-line and batch parts of the system. The ISE Library volume: *Estimating*

## Chapter 8
### Estimating SSADM projects using the Mk II Function Point Analysis spreadsheet

*with Mk II Function Point Analysis* includes advice on calculating these figures (see Sections 7.2, 7.3 and 7.4).

At this point the estimator must enter two other parameters that will be used by the spreadsheet in later stages/steps.

The first of these two parameters gives a Scaling Factor dependent on the type of environment in which the system is to be implemented. The Scaling Factor is used in Stage 2, Step 1, in the formula to calculate productivity.

There are two ways in which the Scaling Factor may be arrived at. The estimator may either enter whether the system is to be implemented using a 4GL or 3GL, in which case the spreadsheet determines the scaling factor to be used. See Section 5.2, Step 1 of the ISE Library volume: the scaling factor is referred to as **A**.

Alternatively, the estimator may directly enter a locally determined scaling factor.

In the row titled 'Enter – 3GL or 4GL (A)' there are two cells into which scaling factor information may be entered. In the column headed 'System Type' the estimator may enter either '3GL' or '4GL' as appropriate. The spreadsheet will then enter the relevant factor, in the next column, headed 'Scaling Factor'.

Alternatively, the estimator may enter a locally determined value for the scaling factor in the column headed 'Local SF', which will then be used in the calculation. Note that if both the 'System Type' and 'Local SF' are entered the figure in the 'Local SF' will take precedence and be used in the calculation.

The second parameter indicates whether the system is on-line, batch or mixed. In the row titled 'Enter – Batch, OL or Mixed', in the column headed 'System Type', the estimator must enter one of the following values, 'Batch', 'OL' or 'Mixed'. The spreadsheet will then generate the appropriate scaling factor in the next column, which is headed 'Scaling Factor'. This scaling factor is used in

Stage 2, Step 2. See Section 5.2, Step 2 of the ISE Library volume: this scaling factor is referred to as **B**.

**Step 2 – Calculation of the unadjusted function points**
The estimating spreadsheet calculates the system size in unadjusted function points using the parameters entered by the estimator in Step 1 and industry average weighting factors.

The ISE Library volume: *Estimating with Mk II Function Point Analysis* includes advice on calibrating these weightings (see Section 7.7). If the estimator wishes to use different weightings to those provided with the spreadsheet then the formulae for the two cells, on-line size and batch size, must be amended to reflect the calibrated weightings.

**Step 3 – Enter the degrees of influence**
The estimator enters the degrees of influence for each of the general application characteristics listed. Advice on assessing the degree of influence for each characteristic is given in the ISE Library volume: *Estimating with Mk II Function Point Analysis* (see Section 7.5). Notice that if no degrees of influence are entered the technical complexity adjustment will be the lowest possible and the project will be treated as the simplest type of project for estimating purposes.

**Step 4 – Calculation of Technical Complexity Adjustment (TCA)**
Once the degrees of influence have been entered the TCA is calculated by the spreadsheet using two industry average constants, 0.65 and 0.005, and the total of the degrees of influence input by the estimator. The coefficient 0.005 may be calibrated, the constant 0.65 is fixed. Advice on calibration is given in the ISE Library volume: *Estimating with Mk II Function Point Analysis* (see Section 7.8).

**Step 5 – Calculation of on-line and batch system sizes**
The size of the on-line and the batch parts of the system are calculated in Mk II function points by the spreadsheet.

**Step 6 – Calculation of total system size**
The total system size in Mk II function points is calculated by the spreadsheet by summing the on-line and batch sizes calculated in Step 5.

8.4.2 Stage 2 – Calculate the normative effort and elapsed time

**Step 1 – Calculation of productivity**
The estimator will already have entered information from which a scaling factor for the implementation environment is derived (see Stage 1, Step 1). This scaling factor is used in the formula to calculate productivity.

**Step 2 – Calculation of effort**
The estimator will already have entered information about the type of system, ie whether it is batch, on-line or mixed (see Stage 1, Step 1). This information is used by the spreadsheet at this point to calculate the normative effort in work hours that one would expect on average for the size of project and type of environment, given the productivity calculated in Stage 2, Step 1.

**Step 3 – Calculation of delivery rate**
The estimated delivery rate is calculated by the spreadsheet using a formula defining the size-delivery relationship. The size-delivery relationship has been arrived at from measurements taken from a large number of projects. The spreadsheet calculation may be checked by reference to the graph provided as Figure 10 (page 28) of the ISE Library volume *Estimating with Mk II Function Point Analysis*. Delivery rate is the estimated delivery rate per elapsed week.

**Step 4 – Calculation of elapsed time**
The spreadsheet calculates the estimated normative elapsed weeks (not the man-days) for the whole project. The calculation of elapsed time is based on the average normally taken for the size of the system and the project environment. Later the spreadsheet calculates the headcount required to achieve this elapsed time (see Stage 5, Step 4).

8.4.3 Stage 3 – Explode effort and elapsed time by module and phase

As a default the spreadsheet uses percentage profiles based on industry average data. However, if calibration data is available from previous SSADM projects this should be used instead of the default percentages. These percentages should be entered for each module and phase beneath the heading 'User Input Module Percentage Profiles'. If the estimator wishes to enter any locally determined percentages, either for effort or for elapsed time, then an entry must be made for all of the modules/phases in that particular column so that the percentage total for all modules/phases in that column is 100 per cent.

8.4.4 Stage 4 – Consider performance influencing risk factors

**Step 1 – Consider system size**
If the system is significantly larger than those previously developed the estimator may enter a percentage figure to increase the effort and elapsed time figures already calculated.

**Step 2 – Consider positive and negative factors**
*Enter positive factor adjustment percentage*
The project may have positive factors, which mean that the effort and elapsed time estimates can be reduced, eg if the system is a re-implementation of an existing well-documented system. The estimator must consider the impact of these positive factors and enter a percentage by which the effort and elapsed time figures are to be reduced. Note that the percentages input for effort and elapsed time do not have to be the same.

*Enter negative factor adjustment percentage*
The project may have negative factors, so that the effort and elapsed time estimates will need to be increased, eg the user is not committed to the project. If this is the case the estimator must consider the impact, if any, of these negative factors on each module or phase and enter percentages for effort and elapsed time against the modules/phases affected.

**Step 3 – Consider the impact of technology**
The estimator must also consider the impact on the project estimates of the use of new methods, techniques or new technology, which may mean that the effort and elapsed times need to be increased. If there is an impact the estimator must enter percentages for effort and elapsed time against the affected modules/phases.

The spreadsheet takes the percentages entered by the estimator and produces revised estimates of effort and elapsed time for each module/phase.

# Chapter 8
## Estimating SSADM projects using the Mk II Function Point Analysis spreadsheet

8.4.5 Stage 5 – Consider time and manpower constraints

**Step 1 – Calculation of Schedule Compression Factor (SCF)**
If there is a time constraint on the project this is used to calculate the schedule compression factor. The estimator enters the available time in elapsed weeks (excluding holidays, training, sick-leave allowance etc) enabling the SCF to be calculated by the spreadsheet.

**Step 2 – Resulting SCF is less than 0.5**
This step is not included as part of the spreadsheet, but is included here for information. If the SCF calculated is less than 0.5 then the success of the project is at risk and project management should consider the options available to them for reducing the risk. The ISE Library volume: *Estimating with Mk II Function Point Analysis* gives advice on some of the options that might be available, including breaking the project up into sub-projects. If the SCF is less than 0.5 the spreadsheet highlights this fact with a warning message.

**Step 3 – Calculation of new effort and time**
The spreadsheet recalculates the effort and elapsed time figures for each module/phase using the SCF. If no available time is entered by the estimator then the spreadsheet enters the previously calculated figures for effort and elapsed time.

**Step 4 – Compute the required headcount**
The spreadsheet calculates the required headcount in full-time equivalents per module or phase.

**Step 5 – Round headcount figures**
The estimator must enter rounded head count figures for each module or phase in the column headed 'Rounded', so that the figures become reasonable fractions. The spreadsheet recalculates the 'Effort' and 'Elapsed Time' figures to reflect the rounding.

**Step 6 – Adjust elapsed weeks for holidays, etc**
The estimator must adjust the elapsed time calculated in Step 5 to allow for holidays and training courses. These final elapsed time figures must be entered in the column headed 'Adjusted Time'.

# Estimating on an SSADM Project

# Annex A: Estimating points and scope

| Module | Step | Estimating Points ||||||||| 
|        |      | A | B | C | D | E | F | G | H | I |
|--------|------|---|---|---|---|---|---|---|---|---|
| 1: FS  |      |   |   |   |   |   |   |   |   |   |
|        | 010  | p |   |   |   |   |   |   |   |   |
|        | 020  | p | f |   |   |   |   |   |   |   |
|        | 030  | p | f |   |   |   |   |   |   |   |
|        | 040  | p | f | f |   |   |   |   |   |   |
| 2: RA  |      |   |   | f |   |   |   |   |   |   |
|        | 110  |   |   | f | p |   |   |   |   |   |
|        | 120  |   |   | f | p | f |   |   |   |   |
|        | 130  |   |   | f | p | f |   |   |   |   |
|        | 140  |   |   | f | p | f |   |   |   |   |
|        | 150  |   |   | f | p | f |   |   |   |   |
|        | 160  |   |   | f | p | f |   |   |   |   |
|        |      |   |   | f | p | f |   |   |   |   |
|        | 210  |   |   | f | p | f |   |   |   |   |
|        | 220  |   |   | f | p | f | f |   |   |   |
| 3: RS  |      |   |   | p |   | p | f |   |   |   |
|        | 310  |   |   | p |   | p | f |   |   |   |
|        | 320  |   |   | p |   | p | f |   |   |   |
|        | 330  |   |   | p |   | p | f |   |   |   |
|        | 340  |   |   | p |   | p | f |   |   |   |
|        | 350  |   |   | p |   | p | f |   |   |   |
|        | 360  |   |   | p |   | p | f |   |   |   |
|        | 370  |   |   | p |   | p | f |   |   |   |
|        | 380  |   |   | p |   | p | f |   |   |   |
| 4: LSS |      |   |   | p |   | p | p |   |   |   |
|        | 410  |   |   | p |   | p | p |   |   |   |
|        | 420  |   |   | p |   | p | p | f |   |   |
|        |      |   |   | p |   | p | p | f |   |   |
|        | 510  |   |   | p |   | p | p | f |   |   |
|        | 520  |   |   | p |   | p | p | f |   |   |
|        | 530  |   |   | p |   | p | p | f |   |   |
|        | 540  |   |   | p |   | p | p | f |   |   |
| 5: PD  |      |   |   | p |   | p | p | p |   |   |
|        | 610  |   |   | p |   | p | p | p | p |   |
|        | 620  |   |   | p |   | p | p | p | p | f |
|        | 630  |   |   | p |   | p | p | p | p | f |
|        | 640  |   |   | p |   | p | p | p | p | f |
|        | 650  |   |   | p |   | p | p | p | p | f |
|        | 660  |   |   | p |   | p | p | p | p | f |
|        | 670  |   |   | p |   | p | p | p | p | f |

Table A1: Estimating points and scope (p = provisional, f = firm)

# Estimating on an SSADM Project

Underlined estimating points, eg B , are at prescribed planning points in SSADM Version 4. The others are recommended, where a Study is to be undertaken as an administratively distinct project, eg contracted out to a different supplier than the one who carried out the preceding Study or Module.

For example, a prescribed planning point appears at step 020 of a Feasibility Study and this is denoted by estimating point B. Estimating point C takes place at step 040 and covers stages and steps from that point onwards.

The uncertainty attached to provisional estimates should diminish as the project progresses, and more information about the system is available. This applies in particular to the provisional estimates indicated at G and H.

Circumstances may require estimates to be made or revised in between the points shown. The estimating approach to be taken in such cases, and technique(s) used, should be those of the preceding estimating point authorized by project management.

# Annex B: Estimating points

| Estimating Point | Estimate Type | Estimate Scope | Knowns | Unknowns | Type of Technique | Examples |
|---|---|---|---|---|---|---|
| A | Provisional | Feasibility Study | Major objectives, constraints & products; functional boundary | System scope; overview processing, LDS & requirements; extent of study required | Top-down; analogy; non-algorithmic | Ratios; expert judgement |
| B | Firm | Feasibility Study | System scope; overview processing, LDS & requirements; extent of study required | Number of interviews required; complexity of system (current and proposed) | Bottom-up | |
| C | Firm | Requirements Analysis | Major processes, entities & requirements; steps, tasks & products | Iterations of techniques; further requirements | Bottom-up | |
| C (cont.) | Provisional | Requirements Specification; Logical System Specification; Physical Design | As above; also Feasibility Study actual effort/time; Requirement Analysis firm estimate | Number of functions, events & enquiries; other detailed project sizing information | Top-down; algorithmic | Ratios; FPA; Function Weight (System Bangs) |
| D | Provisional | Requirements Analysis | As for A | As for A | As for A | As for A |
| E | Firm | Requirements Analysis | As fro C | As for C | As for C | As for C |
| E (cont.) | Provisional | Requirements Specification; Logical System Specification; Physical Design | As for C | As for C | As for C | As for C |

Table B1: Estimating points

# Estimating on an SSADM Project

| Estimating Point | Estimate Type | Estimate Scope | Knowns | Unknowns | Type of Technique | Examples |
|---|---|---|---|---|---|---|
| F | Firm | Requirements Specification | Chosen BSO; detailed requirements, processes & LDS; steps, tasks & products; Req'ts Analysis actual effort/time | Complexity of functions, ELHs in BSO; Scope/boundary of prototyping; quality of LDM | Bottom-up, also check against top-down | Ratios; FPA (existing system plus req'ts) |
| F (cont.) | Provisional | Logical System Specification; Physical Design | As above; also Req'ts Analysis actual effort/time, Req'ts Spec'n firm estimate | As for C; also the TSO to be chosen is not known | Top-down; algorithmic | Ratios; FPA |
| G | Firm | Logical System Specification | TSO details, incl. number & complexity of functions, events, enquiries & requirements; also Req't Spec'n actual effort/time | | Bottom-up, also top-down | Ratios |
| G (cont.) | Provisional | Physical Design | As above | Performance problems & number of design iterations | As above | As above |
| H | Provisional | Physical Design | Logical System Spec'n details eg updates, enquiries, logical screens; also actual effort/time for all previous modules | As for G | As for G | As for G |
| I | Firm | Physical Design | As for H | As for G | As for G | As for G |

Table B1: Estimating points (continued)

# Annex C: Estimating Spreadsheet

| | | | Expected Range |
|---|---|---|---|
| **PROJECT INITIATION DOCUMENT PARAMETERS** | major system processes | | typically between 1 and 6 |
| | user areas | | typically between 1 and 4 |
| | user view entities | | typically between 10 and 15 |
| | key interviews | | 1 to 3 per user area |
| | major reports | | |

| | | | Default used |
|---|---|---|---|
| **PROJECT CHARACTERISTICS** | percentage new requirements | 50% | default 50% |
| | percentage online | 50% | default 50% |
| | percentage enquiry functions | 30% | default 30% |
| | percentage of dialogues to be prototyped | 50% | default 50% |
| | percentage of reports to be prototyped | 50% | default 50% |
| | number of BSOs | 3 | default 3 (typically between 2 and 4) |
| | number of TSOs | 3 | default 3 (typically between 2 and 4) |

| | | | Suggested default value |
|---|---|---|---|
| **DERIVED PARAMETERS** | support interviews | 0 | key interviews * 2 |
| | level 2 data flow diagrams | 0 | major system processes * 2 |
| | new functions | 0 | level 2 DFDs * 5 * %age new requirements |
| | required functions | 0 | level 2 DFDs * 4 |
| | key functions | 0 | required functions * 3 /10 |
| | LDM entities | 0 | user view entities * 3 |
| | events | 0 | LDM entities * 3 |
| | TNF sources | 0 | required functions * 1.5 |
| | Required System LDM entities | 0 | LDM entities * 4 /3 |
| | TNF submodels | 0 | TNF sources /6 |
| | enquiry functions | 0 | required functions * %age enquiry |
| | enquiries | 0 | enquiry functions + update functions /3 |
| | dialogues | 0 | required functions * %age on-line |
| | key reports | 0 | major reports * %age to be prototyped |
| | key dialogues | 0 | dialogues * %age to be prototyped |

| | | |
|---|---|---|
| ADJUSTMENT FACTOR | | 100% |
| PROJECT COMPLEXITY | (type 1=1; type 2=2; type 3=3) | 1 |

Figure C.1: SSADM project estimates initial parameters

# Estimating on an SSADM Project

**STAGE 1 INVESTIGATION OF CURRENT ENVIRONMENT**

|  |  |  |  |  |  |  |  |  | Unit Days | | |
|---|---|---|---|---|---|---|---|---|---|---|---|
| STEP | DESCRIPTION | Est Unit | Units | Step Cmpx | Days/Unit | Std Days | Adjstd Days | Totals | Type 1 | Type 2 | Type 3 |
| 110 | ESTABLISH ANALYSIS FRAMEWORK | system | 1 | 1 | 8 | 8 | 8 |  | 8 | 10 | 12 |
|  |  | key intvw | 0 |  | 3 | 0 | 0 |  | 3 | 3 | 3 |
|  |  | sup intvw | 0 |  | 0.5 | 0 | 0 |  | 0.5 | 0.65 | 0.8 |
|  |  |  |  |  |  | subtotal |  | 8 |  |  |  |
| 120 | INVESTIGATE AND DEFINE REQUIREMENTS | user area | 0 | 1 | 1 | 0 | 0 |  | 1 | 1.2 | 1.5 |
|  |  | lev 2 DFD | 0 |  | 0.5 | 0 | 0 |  | 0.5 | 0.75 | 1 |
|  |  |  |  |  |  | subtotal |  | 0 |  |  |  |
| 130 | INVESTIGATE CURRENT PROCESSING | user area | 0 | 1 | 1 | 0 | 0 |  | 1 | 2 | 3 |
|  |  | lev 2 DFD | 0 |  | 1 | 0 | 0 |  | 1 | 1.3 | 2 |
|  |  |  |  |  |  | subtotal |  | 0 |  |  |  |
| 140 | INVESTIGATE CURRENT DATA | entity | 0 | 1 | 0.15 | 0 | 0 |  | 0.15 | 0.22 | 0.4 |
|  |  | lev 2 DFD | 0 |  | 0.5 | 0 | 0 |  | 0.5 | 0.5 | 0.5 |
|  |  |  |  |  |  | subtotal |  | 0 |  |  |  |
| 150 | DERIVE LOGICAL VIEW OF CURRENT SERVICES | user area | 0 | 1 | 1 | 0 | 0 |  | 1 | 2 | 3 |
|  |  | lev 2 DFD | 0 |  | 1 | 0 | 0 |  | 1 | 1.2 | 1.8 |
|  |  |  |  |  |  | subtotal |  | 0 |  |  |  |
| 160 | ASSEMBLE INVESTIGATION RESULTS | system | 1 | 1 | 3 | 3 | 3 |  | 3 | 5 | 8 |
|  |  |  |  |  |  | subtotal |  | 3 |  |  |  |
|  |  |  |  |  |  | total |  | 11 |  |  |  |
|  |  |  |  |  |  | user contact |  | 0 |  |  |  |

Figure C.2: RA Requirements Analysis Module

# Annex C
Estimating spreadsheet

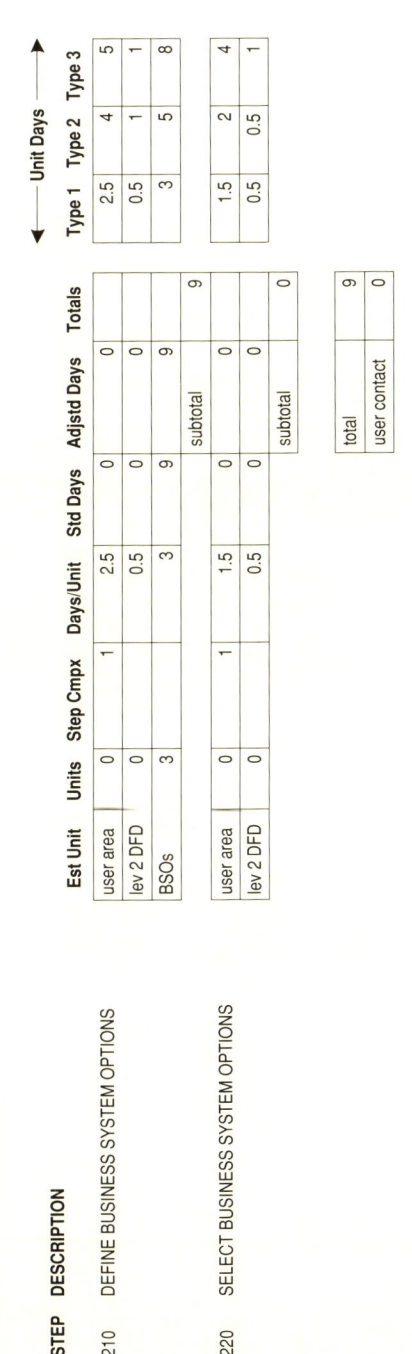

Figure C.3: RA Requirements Analysis Module (continued)

# Estimating on an SSADM Project

**STAGE 3 DEFINITION OF REQUIREMENTS**

| STEP | DESCRIPTION | Est Unit | Units | Step Cmpx | Days/Unit | Std Days | Adjstd Days | Totals | Type 1 | Type 2 | Type 3 |
|---|---|---|---|---|---|---|---|---|---|---|---|
| 310 | DEFINE REQUIRED SYSTEM PROCESSING | new funcs | 0 | 1 | 1 | 0 | 0 | | 1 | 1.5 | 2 |
| | | req funcs | 0 | | 0.15 | 0 | 0 | | 0.15 | 0.18 | 0.22 |
| | | lev 2 DFD | 0 | | 0.2 | 0 | 0 | subtotal 0 | 0.2 | 0.25 | 0.35 |
| 320 | DEVELOP REQUIRED DATA MODEL | new funcs | 0 | 1 | 0.5 | 0 | 0 | | 0.5 | 0.5 | 0.5 |
| | | lev 2 DFD | 0 | | 0.2 | 0 | 0 | subtotal 0 | 0.2 | 0.25 | 0.35 |
| 330 | DERIVE SYSTEM FUNCTIONS | user area | 0 | 1 | 1 | 0 | 0 | | 1 | 2 | 4 |
| | | req funcs | 0 | | 0.5 | 0 | 0 | subtotal 0 | 0.5 | 0.6 | 0.8 |
| 340 | ENHANCE REQUIRED DATA MODEL | inf source | 0 | 1 | 0.15 | 0 | 0 | | 0.15 | 0.2 | 0.2 |
| | | inf submdl | 0 | | 1 | 0 | 0 | | 1 | 1 | 1 |
| | | system | 1 | | 1 | 1 | 1 | subtotal 1 | 1 | 2 | 3 |
| 350 | DEVELOP SPECIFICATION PROTOTYPES | user area | 0 | 1 | 1 | 0 | 0 | | 1 | 1 | 2 |
| | | key dials | 0 | | 3 | 0 | 0 | | 3 | 3 | 4 |
| | | key repts | 0 | | 0.5 | 0 | 0 | subtotal 0 | 0.5 | 0.5 | 0.5 |
| 360 | DEVELOP PROCESSING SPECIFICATION | entity | 0 | 1 | 1 | 0 | 3 | | 1 | 1 | 1.5 |
| | | event | 0 | | 0.25 | 0 | 3 | | 0.25 | 0.3 | 0.4 |
| | | enquiries | 0 | | 0.25 | 0 | 3 | subtotal 0 | 0.25 | 0.25 | 0.25 |
| 370 | CONFIRM SYSTEM OBJECTIVES | user area | 0 | 1 | 2 | 0 | 0 | subtotal 0 | 2 | 3 | 4 |
| 380 | ASSEMBLE REQUIREMENTS SPECIFICATION | user area | 0 | 1 | 4 | 0 | 0 | | 4 | 5 | 6 |

Unit Days — Type 1 / Type 2 / Type 3

| | |
|---|---|
| total | 1 |
| user contact | 0 |

Figure C.4: RS Requirements Specification Module

Annex C
Estimating spreadsheet

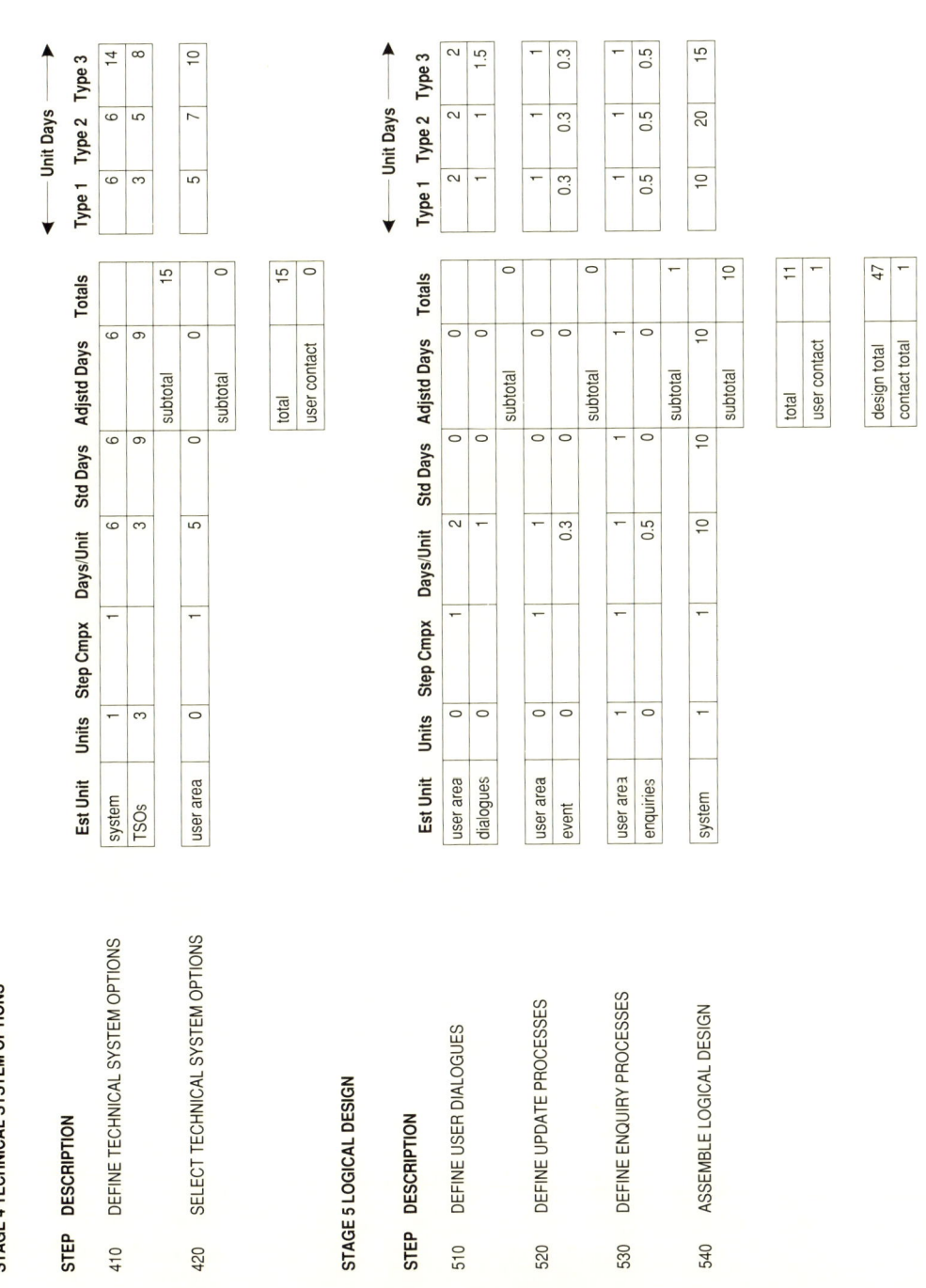

Figure C.5: LS Logical System Specification Module

91

# Estimating on an SSADM Project

# Annex D: Mk II Function Point Analysis spreadsheet

**Stage 1 - Assess the system size in Mk II function points**

Step 1    Enter the total attribute and entity parameters

|  | On-line | Batch |
|---|---|---|
| total number of input attribute types (NI) |  |  |
| total number of entity types (NER) |  |  |
| total number of output attribute types (NO) |  |  |

|  | System Type | Scaling Factor | Local SF |
|---|---|---|---|
| Enter - 3GL or 4GL (A) |  | 0.00 |  |
| Enter - Batch, OL, Mixed (B) |  | 0.00 |  |

Step 2    Calculation of unadjusted function points

| System size in unadjusted function points | 0.00 | 0.00 |
|---|---|---|

Step 3    Enter the degrees of influence

|  | On-line | Batch |
|---|---|---|
| Data communication | 0 | 0 |
| Distributed function | 0 | 0 |
| Performance | 0 | 0 |
| Heavily used configuration | 0 | 0 |
| Transaction rates | 0 | 0 |
| On-line data entry | 0 | 0 |
| Design for end-user efficiency | 0 | 0 |
| On-line update | 0 | 0 |
| Complex processing | 0 | 0 |
| Usable in other applications | 0 | 0 |
| Installation ease | 0 | 0 |
| Operations ease | 0 | 0 |
| Multiple sites | 0 | 0 |
| Facilitate change | 0 | 0 |
| Requirements of other applications | 0 | 0 |
| Security, privacy, audit | 0 | 0 |
| User training needed | 0 | 0 |
| Direct use by third parties | 0 | 0 |
| Documentation | 0 | 0 |

# Estimating on an SSADM Project

**Step 4**  Calculation of Technical Complexity Adjustment

|  | On-line | Batch |
|---|---|---|
| Technical Complexity Adjustment | 0.65 | 0.65 |

**Step 5**  Calculation of on-line and batch system sizes

|  | On-line | Batch |
|---|---|---|
| Adjusted system size | 0.00 | 0.00 |

**Step 6**  Calculation of total system size

| Total system size - batch plus on-line (S) | 0.00 |
|---|---|

## Stage 2 - Calculate the normative effort and elapsed time

**Step 1**  Calculation of Productivity

| Estimated productivity (P) | 0.00 |
|---|---|

**Step 2**  Calculation of effort

| Estimated effort in work-hours | 0.00 |
|---|---|

**Step 3**  Calculation of delivery rate

| Estimated delivery rate (D) | 0.00 |
|---|---|

**Step 4**  Calculation of elapsed time

| Estimated elapsed time in weeks | 0.00 |
|---|---|

## Stage 3 - Explode effort and elapsed time by module and phase

| User Input Module Percentage Profiles | | |
|---|---|---|
|  | Effort | Elapsed Time |
| Requirements Analysis |  |  |
| Requirements Specification |  |  |
| Logical System Specification |  |  |
| Physical Design |  |  |
| Code and Unit Test |  |  |
| System Test |  |  |
| Implementation |  |  |

# Annex D
## Mk II Function Point Analysis spreadsheet

|  | Effort | Elapsed Time |
|---|---|---|
| Requirements Analysis | 0.00 | 0.00 |
| Requirements Specification | 0.00 | 0.00 |
| Logical System Specification | 0.00 | 0.00 |
| Physical Design | 0.00 | 0.00 |
| Code and Unit Test | 0.00 | 0.00 |
| System Test | 0.00 | 0.00 |
| Implementation | 0.00 | 0.00 |

**Stage 4 - Consider performance influencing risk factors**

Step 1

| Consider system size | Effort | Elapsed Time |
|---|---|---|
| Enter system size adjustment %age | | |

Step 2

| Consider positive and negative factors | Effort | Elapsed Time |
|---|---|---|
| Enter positive factor adjustment %age | | |
| | | |
| Enter negative factor adjustment %age | | |
| • Requirements Analysis | | |
| • Requirements Specification | | |
| • Logical System Specification | | |
| • Physical Design | | |
| • Code and Unit Test | | |
| • System Test | | |
| • Implementation | | |

Step 3

| Consider the impact of technology | Effort | Elapsed Time |
|---|---|---|
| Enter technical innovation adjustment %age | | |
| • Requirements Analysis | | |
| • Requirements Specification | | |
| • Logical System Specification | | |
| • Physical Design | | |
| • Code and Unit Test | | |
| • System Test | | |
| • Implementation | | |

# Estimating on an SSADM Project

| Recalculated effort and elapsed time | Effort | Elapsed Time |
|---|---|---|
| • Requirements Analysis | 0.00 | 0.00 |
| • Requirements Specification | 0.00 | 0.00 |
| • Logical System Specification | 0.00 | 0.00 |
| • Physical Design | 0.00 | 0.00 |
| • Code and Unit Test | 0.00 | 0.00 |
| • System Test | 0.00 | 0.00 |
| • Implementation | 0.00 | 0.00 |

| New total effort and elapsed time | 0.00 | 0.00 |
|---|---|---|

## Stage 5 - Consider time and manpower constraints

**Step 1**     Calculation of schedule compression factor

| Enter available time in weeks | |
|---|---|
| Schedule compression factor (SCF) | 0.00 |

**Step 3**     Calculation of new effort and time

| Calculation of new effort and time | Effort | Elapsed Time |
|---|---|---|
| Compressed effort and new elapsed time | 0.00 | 0.00 |
| • Requirements Analysis | 0.00 | 0.00 |
| • Requirements Specification | 0.00 | 0.00 |
| • Logical System Specification | 0.00 | 0.00 |
| • Physical Design | 0.00 | 0.00 |
| • Code and Unit Test | 0.00 | 0.00 |
| • System Test | 0.00 | 0.00 |
| • Implementation | 0.00 | 0.00 |

**Step 4**     **Compute the required headcount**

| Compute the required headcount | Headcount |
|---|---|
| Requirements Analysis | 0.00 |
| Requirements Specification | 0.00 |
| Logical System Specification | 0.00 |
| Physical Design | 0.00 |
| Code and Unit Test | 0.00 |
| System Test | 0.00 |
| Implementation | 0.00 |

# Annex D
# Mk II Function Point Analysis spreadsheet

**Step 5** **Round headcount figures**

| Enter rounded headcount | | | |
|---|---|---|---|
| | Rounded | Effort | Elapsed time |
| Requirements Analysis | | | |
| Requirements Specification | | | |
| Logical System Specification | | | |
| Physical Design | | | |
| Code and Unit Test | | | |
| System Test | | | |
| Implementation | | | |
| Total Recalculated Effort and Elapsed Time | | 0.00 | 0.00 |

**Step 6** **Adjust elapsed weeks for holidays, etc**

| Enter adjusted elapsed weeks | |
|---|---|
| | Adjusted Time |
| Requirements Analysis | |
| Requirements Specification | |
| Logical System Specification | |
| Physical Design | |
| Code and Unit Test | |
| System Test | |
| Implementation | |

97

# Estimating on an SSADM Project

# Bibliography

The following CCTA and other products are either directly referred to or expand on the topics discussed in this volume.

**Information Systems Engineering Library**

The Information Systems Engineering Library volumes are available from HMSO Bookshops and the HMSO Publications Centre, PO Bos 276, London SW8 5DT, telephone 0171 873 9090 or fax 0171 873 8200.

- Estimating with MK II Function Point Analysis
  ISBN 0 946683 53 0

**SSADM**

The set of 4 SSADM Manuals are available from NCC Blackwell, Oxford House, Oxford Road, Manchester M1 7ED.

- SSADM Version 4
  ISBN 1 85554 004 5

**Other publications**

Cost Estimation for Software Development, B Londeix, Addison–Wesley,
ISBN 0 201 17451 0, 1987

Function Point Analysis, J B Dreger, Prentice Hall,
ISBN 0 13 332321 8, 1989

Software Engineering Economics, B W Boehm, Prentice Hall, 1981

Software Metrics, T Gilb, Chartwell-Bratt Ltd., 1976

Software Sizing and Estimating, Mk II Function Point Analysis, C R Symons, John Wiley and Sons Ltd.,
ISBN 0 471 92985 9, 1991

# Estimating on an SSADM Project

# Glossary

This glossary only contains terms used in the body of the volume. It is not intended as a comprehensive glossary of all terms and techniques that may be encountered in estimating literature.

**Algorithmic Model**  An instance of an algorithmic approach to estimating, ie one that employs a specific formula or set of formulae to calculate the estimates.

**Analogy**  The use of historic data about projects to support estimating. Data may be installation-specific or industry figures, and may be structured more or less formally (ie recollection or written notes are as much instances of analogy as the use of a formal database).

**Calibration**  The setting in an estimating workbench/support tool of reference values based on the project experience of the specific user installation.

**Confidence levels/limits**  The margins of error deemed to attach to an estimate, due to risk and uncertainty factors; normally expressed as a percentage.

**Constraint model**  An instance of an algorithmic model that allows constraints (eg time or resource limitations) to be taken into account in the estimation process.

**Contingency**  Provision in project plans to cover factors that cannot be accurately identified or assessed at the estimation stage.

**Estimate**  A statement of the amount of work, resource and timescale required to achieve the development of a product or system to an agreed level of quality, together with the confidence limits attached to the estimates to allow for the risk factors.

**Estimating Model**  The process of arriving at a set of project estimates.

**Estimating/estimation point**  A defined point in the development cycle where estimates should be prepared/revised.

| | |
|---|---|
| **Firm estimate** | An estimate with the minimum achievable confidence limits attached; required at least for the stage or module that succeeds the current estimation point. |
| **Function Point Analysis** | An estimating technique designed to assess a project in terms of the functionality to be delivered by the system to the user. |
| **Informal estimating** | Approaches to estimating that do not necessarily require the application of a formally prescribed method. |
| **Intuitive estimating** | Approaches to estimating that are based on individual experience, and cannot necessarily be justified by reference to specific documented figures or calculations. |
| **Metric** | Any variable pertaining to estimating that can be measured. |
| **Module** | In the SSADM context, a defined subset of the development cycle for project planning and hence for estimating purposes. |
| **Product-based estimating** | Estimating based on the time/effort required to produce each deliverable/product defined for a project. |
| **Project Model** | The set of activities to be carried out on a project and products that are to be produced by the project. |
| **Provisional estimate** | An estimate accommodating broad confidence limits; typically to cover those parts of the development cycle that follow the part for which there is currently a Firm Estimate. |
| **Putnam/Norden/Rayleigh technique** | A technique embodying a model based on a specific distribution of effort across the development cycle, with system size being represented in terms of lines of code. |
| **Risk** | In the context of this volume, a factor deriving from the nature of the system under development which may detract from the reliability of any estimate for the relevant part(s) of the project; a risk should be allowed for in estimates through the retention of confidence limits on the relevant estimate(s). |

# Glossary

| | |
|---|---|
| **Scheduling** | The process of mapping project tasks against time and resources. |
| **Stage** | Development stage: a subset of the activities and products in the development cycle that is defined by the relevant development methodology. |
| | Project management stage: a subset of the activities and products in the development cycle that is defined for project management purposes. |
| **Stage ratio** | A statement of the percentages of a development project that are typically attributable to each stage (usually interpreted as development stage). |
| **Step** | The level below a stage employed in project planning and hence in estimating. |
| **System Bangs** | An estimating technique based on the assessment of a system in terms of its activities and entities. |
| **System Model** | The technical content of a system under development. |
| **Task-based estimating** | Estimating based on the time/effort required for each task defined for a project. |
| **Uncertainty** | A factor deriving from the lack of detailed information about one or more areas of the Project Model or System Model that detracts from the reliability of any estimate for the relevant part(s) of the project; uncertainty should be allowed for in estimates through the allowance of confidence limits on the relevant estimate(s). |

# Estimating on an SSADM Project